D1625307

KEYNES

BY THE SAME AUTHOR

The Last Thousand Days of the British Empire
The Keynesian Revolution in the Making, 1924–1936
Hope and Glory, Britain 1900–2000
The Cripps Version: The Life of Sir Stafford Cripps
A Question of Leadership: Gladstone to Blair
The Keynesian Revolution and its Economic Consequences
Liberals and Social Democrats
Lancashire and the New Liberalism

KEYNES

The Twentieth Century's
Most Influential Economist

PETER CLARKE

BLOOMSBURY

LONDON · BERLIN · NEW YORK

First published in Great Britain 2009

Copyright © 2009 by Peter Clarke

The moral right of the author has been asserted

No part of this book may be used or reproduced in any manner
whatsoever without written permission from the Publisher except in the
case of brief quotations embodied in critical articles or reviews

Every reasonable effort has been made to trace copyright holders of
material reproduced in this book, but if any have been inadvertently
overlooked the Publishers would be glad to hear from them

Bloomsbury Publishing Plc
36 Soho Square
London W1D 3QY

www.bloomsbury.com

Bloomsbury Publishing, London, New York and Berlin
A CIP catalogue record for this book is available from the British Library

ISBN 978 1 4088 0385 1

10 9 8 7 6 5 4 3 2 1

Typeset by Hewer Text UK Ltd, Edinburgh
Printed in Great Britain by Clays Limited, St Ives plc

Mixed Sources
Product group from well-managed
forests and other controlled sources
www.fsc.org Cert no. SGS-COC-2061
© 1996 Forest Stewardship Council
FSC

In the long run, for my grandchildren

CONTENTS

Introduction

A Roller-coaster Reputation

W HAT IF THE world is in depression – again? Any talk of a 'slowdown' now seems risible. Talk of a possible 'technical recession' has come and gone. Even sound bites about the 'credit crunch' do not measure up. 'Recession' has been officially acknowledged – meaning at least two consecutive quarters of decline – in one after another of the major economies. So we have become accustomed to the phrase, from economists, business leaders and politicians alike, that this looks like the worst scenario 'since the Great Depression of the 1930s'. But what if this is actually a depression of that magnitude? Whatever can we do about it? How on earth can we understand it?

We can start by learning from what happened before. If we are short of ideas ourselves, we may have a new interest in the ideas that came out of the last epoch of depression, unemployment and uncertainty. One name above all keeps on cropping up, not only when economists discuss the situation but in the columns of British and North American newspapers and magazines, and in other media commentary. Often there is a grainy picture of a tall, stooped man with a pasty face, watery eyes, thinning hair and a heavy moustache, a half-familiar figure from a former era of worldwide economic depression – an era that closed when the Second World

War peremptorily intervened. It's Keynes, of course. But who was he and why does his thinking matter to us now?

His is an extraordinary reputation. Through nine decades, he has been celebrated, scorned, respected, appropriated, mocked, venerated, derided, rediscovered – but seldom ignored. The name of John Maynard Keynes first came to wide public attention, on both sides of the Atlantic, in 1920. Still under forty, he became famous not as an academic economist but as the author of a sparkling and influential tract, published in London just before Christmas 1919. *The Economic Consequences of the Peace* focused public opinion on the defects of the recent Versailles Peace Treaty. Its account had an I-was-there immediacy, a magisterial detachment and a compelling plausibility. Had the British war leader Lloyd George, in his wily Welsh way, really 'bamboozled' the upright Presbyterian President Woodrow Wilson about the impossible reparations demanded of the defeated Germans? For when Keynes dramatised the salient issues, this is how he cast the key figures and brought them to life. What he hoped to do for his readers – and what he charged a belatedly penitent Lloyd George with failing to do for the sadly deceived President – was to 'de-bamboozle' them about what had really been going on behind the scenes.

The Economic Consequences of the Peace, a slim and readable volume, rapidly became an international bestseller. By April 1920, 18,500 copies had been sold in Britain. This was extremely good for a hardback by a hitherto unknown author, whose name had only crept into the small print of the London newspapers the previous year as one of Lloyd George's Treasury aides at the Paris peace conference: an obscure Brit with a walk-on role in the negotiations, who appeared for the first time in the *New York Times* of 27 May 1919 as 'John M. Keynes' – a form of his name that he never used. Yet, within a year, the American edition of *The Economic Consequences of the Peace* had sold 70,000 copies and the *New York Times* had given a full-page review to a book that was to be roundly denounced almost as often as it was eagerly purchased: 'in the English-speaking countries it is capable of doing immense mischief by still further clouding the issues of an epoch already sufficiently turbid.'[1]

Keynes's capacity for immense mischief, far from being exhausted by this episode, was only just beginning. He had entered the world stage with a fanfare, prepared to brave the boos and catcalls of a hostile audience if need be, and he subsequently remained in the spotlight, not least in the United States. In London, he was to be mentioned in *The Times* in about sixty reports or editorials during the 1920s, and in about a hundred during the 1930s. Across the Atlantic, by comparison, his name appeared in the *New York Times* nearly 300 times in the 1920s – a raft of references to a man whose subsequent career Americans followed with evident attention. Thus when the author of *The Economic Consequences of the Peace*, later in the 1920s, turned his lively mind and his deadly pen to the problem of unemployment, he already had a platform and an audience on both sides of the Atlantic.

Conditions in the stagnant British industrial system, however, were far different from those in the buoyant American economy, at least until the 1929 crash. As an economist based in the University of Cambridge, Keynes was naturally concerned primarily with the symptoms of depression in his own country. Conservatives liked to claim that protectionism offered a promising alternative, especially if tariffs could be used to bind together the British Empire. Like most economists, Keynes did not take this line, but nor was he happy with an orthodoxy that simply relied on market forces to do the trick. Instead, he boldly entered public debate with the contention that unemployment needed a drastic remedy.

Curiously, the politician whom he was supporting by the mid-1920s was none other than Lloyd George. 'The man who won the war', as propaganda for his coalition government had dubbed him in 1918, was the same man who lost the peace in 1919 – or so *The Economic Consequences of the Peace* had famously argued. Lloyd

George was now attempting a comeback, having himself come back to a reunited Liberal Party, of which Keynes was an active member. 'Has Mr Keynes's opinion of Mr Lloyd George's character changed since 1918?' was the inevitable awkward question at one public meeting. 'The difference between me and some other people,' Keynes suavely replied, 'is that I oppose Mr Lloyd George when he is wrong and support him when he is right.'[2] It was one among many subsequent occasions on which he was challenged for inconsistency. He never apologised for changing his mind when confronted by different facts or persuaded by better arguments.

Still the *enfant terrible*, then, Keynes made himself the spokesman for administering a stimulus when the economy was underperforming. We can see it as the launch of a Keynesian agenda that is still debated today. He called the prevailing system one of 'individualism and laissez-faire' and attacked it accordingly. Laissez-faire, said Keynes, had done its work. He claimed that it now meant superstitious faith in the market as an end in itself, whereas the actual situation cried out for experimental devices as a means of promoting recovery. In the Britain of the mid-1920s this orthodoxy relied on the self-acting mechanisms of the Gold Standard and Free Trade to do the trick – in the long run.

No, said Keynes, coining one of his most famous phrases: '*In the long run* we are all dead.'[3] It was a phrase that he was not to be allowed to forget, if only because opponents have always seized on it to show his alleged preoccupation with the short run. As Margaret Thatcher once commented to the Conservative Party conference: 'Anyone who thought like that would never plant a tree.'[4] Keynes's policies can thus be damned out of his own mouth as short-term expedients that saddle future generations with the inexorable costs of defying the market.

Such arguments came to a head with the decision to put Britain back on the Gold Standard in 1925. Winston Churchill was responsible for this, as Chancellor of the Exchequer. As a layman, he struggled to find his way through a technical argument that he recognised as central to the way that the economy worked. He argued and he listened. Keynes's advice was politely listened to; then politely dismissed. The return to gold meant that the pound sterling was, in effect, shackled to an exchange rate of US$4.86. To Churchill, this meant being shackled to realities. To Keynes, the new parity was both completely unrealistic and perfectly avoidable, as was implied by the title of his polemical pamphlet: 'The Economic Consequences of Mr Churchill' (1925).

As a polemicist, Keynes was already fighting in a big league. His advocacy of public works in Britain, in a campaign where he publicly backed Lloyd George, did not find electoral favour in 1929, but later that year, when depression caught up with the American economy too, his arguments could not be ignored. He seized his opportunities to give copious advice to the British Government. Again he persisted; again the Treasury resisted. One of his own closest collaborators, the Liberal economist Hubert Henderson, turned on Keynes at this juncture, accusing him of minimising budget difficulties, with the icy taunt: 'I suggest that you are in great danger, if you persist in ignoring the latter question, and implying that capital expenditure can put it right, of going down to history as the man who persuaded the British people to ruin themselves by gambling on a greater illusion than any of those which he had shattered.'[5]

Keynes was unabashed. He went from bad to worse in the eyes of such critics when he showed himself ready to question, not just the Gold Standard and the sanctity of a balanced budget, but the good old Liberal doctrine of Free Trade too. He tried many tacks, whether resourcefully or inconsistently. 'Where five economists are gathered together,' so government officials now told each other, 'there will be six conflicting opinions and two of them will be held by Keynes!'[6] None of his bright ideas appealed to the Treasury, either under the minority Labour Government which took office from 1929, or under its Conservative-dominated successor, the National Government, which replaced it in the crisis of 1931. Neville Chamberlain, first as Chancellor of the Exchequer and later as Prime Minister, was himself an obvious check on the adoption of a Keynesian agenda.

This 'world economic blizzard', as it was aptly termed, knocked Britain off the Gold Standard in September 1931 and swept away Labour and Liberals alike in a subsequent general election. Keynes had thus lost his most sympathetic potential allies in recruiting political support. An expert in losing friends through his own clever remarks, he managed to turn Lloyd George himself into an antagonist by publishing witty passages that he had prudently omitted from *The Economic Consequences of the Peace*. Hence the inevitable retaliation in Lloyd George's widely read *War Memoirs* (1933) calling Keynes 'an entertaining economist whose bright but shallow dissertations on finance and political economy, when not taken seriously, always provide a source of innocent merriment to his readers'.[7] When even his most prominent champion spoke in such terms, Keynes's political stock in Britain was evidently not riding high at the end of 1933, any more than the international economy itself.

'Say not, the struggle naught availeth', so we have it on poetic authority, with the final reassurance: 'But westward, look, the land is bright.' It was a moment when a new president had taken office in Washington. It was a moment of hope, a time for audacity. In the early months nobody could be sure if this untried Democratic administration knew what it was doing, still less if the measures that it produced would achieve their desired effect. There was an enormous burden of expectation upon the President himself and upon his ability to communicate the thrust of his policies to an anxious public in dire need of reassurance. And he spoke not just to Americans but to a world mired in depression.

What soon became clear was that Franklin D. Roosevelt opted for an active policy, even when it meant disrupting the deliberations of the world economic conference summoned in the summer of 1933. Following the United States's departure from the Gold Standard, a blunt presidential message rejected the 'old fetishes of so-called international bankers', to the predictable consternation of all those who wanted to resurrect the old system. 'It is a long time since a statesman has cut through the cob-webs as boldly as the President of the United States cut through them yesterday', Keynes proclaimed immediately in a widely reported newspaper article, saying that Roosevelt was 'magnificently right in forcing a decision between two widely divergent policies'.[8]

Little wonder that Keynes's name became associated with the policies of the New Deal. In the *New York Times* his name was mentioned nearly 400 times in the 1930s and nearly 500 in the 1940s. Such references were not always in flattering terms, with ideological opponents denouncing him as the evil genius of an experiment allegedly heading towards socialism. The way that Keynes put it himself was set out in an open letter to the President, published in the *New York Times* on the last day of 1933. 'You have made yourself the trustee for those in every country who seek to mend the evils of our condition by reasoned experiment within the framework of the existing social system,' Keynes told Roosevelt. 'If you fail, rational change will be gravely prejudiced throughout the world, leaving orthodoxy and revolution to fight it out.'[9]

The odd fact is that Keynes was not only more central to the American debates about economic policy than he was in his own country during the 1930s, but also more pivotal than any American economist. This was not because the universities of the United States were lacking in theoretical economists of established reputation, or that their credentials were regarded as inferior to those of Keynes. Almost the reverse is true. Until 1936, when he published *The General Theory of Employment, Interest and Money*, Keynes's curriculum vitae looked a little thin if measured against the heavyweight academic contributions of some of his international rivals. The explanation surely lies elsewhere.

Take the example of a great economist, born in the same year as Keynes: Joseph Schumpeter, famous subsequently for his influential concept of 'creative destruction' as the means by which capitalism renews itself. Schumpeter was installed at Harvard in the 1930s – yet his own students seemed more fascinated by the theoretical insights that Keynes was now known to be preaching in his lectures in faraway Cambridge. One effect was that the publication of the *General Theory* was already an event before the event, not least in the other Cambridge, where Harvard students of Schumpeter himself were among those queuing up for their copies. Schumpeter's criticism was that the *General Theory* 'pleads for a definite policy, and on every page the ghost of that policy looks over the shoulder of the analyst, frames his assumptions, guides his pen'.[10]

That was no impediment to eager students, often thirsty to imbibe new doctrines with immediate tonic effect. 'As with the Bible and Marx,' the young Harvard economist J. K. Galbraith was to comment later, 'obscurity stimulated abstract debate.'[11] Hence the tragic moment in 1939 when Schumpeter had finally published his own two scholarly volumes, *Business Cycles*, totalling 1,095 pages. At Harvard, a special seminar on this text was organised by his loyal students – or insufficiently loyal, as it turned out. When it met, the ghastly realisation dawned that nobody had read *Business Cycles*; worse, that they had all read the *General Theory*; worse still, that everyone was talking about Keynes and not about Schumpeter.

True, the reception of Keynes's thinking depended partly on its context, which needs to be understood. And this context includes 'Bloomsbury' – a district of London that became a code name for the cultural milieu in which Keynes moved. It was known well enough in his lifetime that he was close to Lytton Strachey, whose iconoclastic book *Eminent Victorians* had taken the literary world by storm in 1918 – though much about their relationship remained unsaid until later. Likewise, Keynes was a friend of two of the most esteemed novelists of their generation, E. M. Forster and Virginia Woolf. The Bloomsbury connection points to the simple fact – to which we shall need to return – that the impact of Keynes's writings reflected his own skills as a writer.

In Britain, the late 1930s saw the political ascendancy of Neville Chamberlain: hardly good news for John Maynard Keynes. The career trajectory of the Cambridge economist, however, was transformed by the coming of the Second World War, especially the crisis of the summer of 1940, when Britain was pitted in a struggle for national survival under the leadership of Winston Churchill.

It was now that Keynes came to exert hands-on political influence in providing the sinews of war. Suddenly he was no longer just an academic, however famous, but became a policy-maker himself, in the highest echelon of the British Treasury. To anyone who asked exactly what was his job description, the only reply was that he was 'just Keynes'. He enjoyed unique prestige; he became Lord Keynes of Tilton in 1942; he was given a brief of wide scope in negotiating with the Americans, who alone commanded the resources to sustain the British war effort. First there was the flow of wartime aid under the Lend-Lease agreements; then, with the abrupt end of hostilities in 1945, Keynes negotiated a large dollar loan aimed at floating the British economy through the transition to peacetime conditions.

These American commitments were, as Keynes kept acknowledging, generous transactions. But this was not a zero-sum game in which Britain's gain was America's loss. The provoking fact was that the war had created boom times for the American economy, and that Keynesian policies were often and rather indiscriminately credited. It would be going too far to claim that Keynes simply wanted to get his hands on the proceeds of a business that had grown by adopting his own strategy; but he could argue in good faith that Americans were not impoverished by their munificence.

In his ideal world, like that of Adam Smith in the late eighteenth century, everyone stood to benefit from a division of labour, in peace as in war. Enlightened self-interest was the bedrock of Keynes's thinking on international policy. His name was prominently linked with the institution of the Bretton Woods financial system, as set up in 1946, under which, for a quarter of a century after the Second World War, the western world prospered.

In Britain, Churchill's wartime coalition government committed itself to maintaining 'a high and stable level of employment'. In the immediate postwar period, the Keynesian logic of this policy gained bi-partisan acceptance. This was partly through a competitive desire between the parties to disavow responsibility for the mass unemployment in the 1930s – a problem to which the solution seemed so obvious in retrospect, once Keynes had disclosed it. 'The economic ideas of Lord Keynes, which were crystallised very largely as the result of a penetrating analysis of this very situation,' a Conservative Party spokesman explained, as though in apology for Neville Chamberlain's ignorance, 'were not yet matured.' But the crystallisation – 'with which I, as a Conservative, agree' – now made for consensus.[12] 'The effect of Lord Keynes' teaching and the wartime experience,' as a Labour Party spokesman preferred to put it, 'has been the creation of a very widespread belief in Britain that unemployment can be practically prevented by the full development of a planned economy.'[13]

Keynes was active on government business almost until the moment when his heart, which had made him a semi-invalid since 1937, finally succumbed to years of stress in April 1946. 'Appalling news of death of Keynes,' reads the diary entry of one Treasury colleague, Richard ('Otto') Clarke, who had often robustly opposed him. 'Felt bereft, as on the death of Roosevelt.' Friedrich von Hayek, Keynes's most formidable academic opponent, wrote that 'he was the one really great man I ever knew, and for whom I felt admiration'. In London, *The Times*, still conscious of itself as the semi-official newspaper of record, offered the judgement:

'To find an economist of comparable influence one would have to go back to Adam Smith.'[14] But would it last? Keynes's personal magnetism was held in awe. Would his economic theories now lapse into a speedy oblivion once their creator had been fittingly given the final honour of commemoration in Westminster Abbey?

On the contrary. In the subsequent two decades the *General Theory* came to acquire scriptural authority. Like scripture, it was more often cited than read; and in contradictory senses too; but it became essential at least to feign respect for its authority. Thus the appropriation of Keynes's name became *de rigueur* in any mainstream discussion of economic problems, not only in the academy but in the public forum. The most influential thinker in the postwar Labour Party, Tony Crosland, spoke for a generation of liberals on both sides of the Atlantic in the 1950s. 'The Keynesian techniques are now well understood,' he assured them, 'and there is no reason to fear a repetition of the New Deal experience of a government with the will to spend its way out of a recession, but frustrated in doing so by faulty knowledge.'[15]

Keynes's apotheosis was already well under way by the time that Roy Harrod published the major biography of his old friend in 1951. For the next generation, as Harrod realised in writing it, this would stand as the essential insider account of the man, the economist and the international economic statesman. As a result, Harrod wrote under constraint. First he had to submit to some censorship of the government documents that he used. Eminent civil servants pored over Harrod's drafts, worried above all about anything that would give offence in the United States, Britain's cold-war ally and still its banker of last resort in a world short of dollars. Harrod faced another dilemma, even worse than whether to publish disrespectful anti-American gibes or reveal a history of radical political sympathies. For what might give more offence in the United States of the McCarthy era than to disclose an even murkier secret – the elite economist as sexual pervert?

Keynes's homosexuality as a young man was not allowed to taint the pages of the official biography. 'I knew most details of his homo-sexual interests,' Harrod wrote later. 'I did not write blatantly about sex in my book, because at that time it would have been unsuitable; but anyone then, who was alive to the existence of homo-sexual proclivities, would have been able to learn the important facts "between the lines" of my book.'[16] As he well knew, his was a story only apparent to a select few who knew it already. Most of his readers, on either side of the Atlantic, saw nothing to disturb their innocence. It was not until Michael Holroyd set off the vogue for big, candid Bloomsbury biographies with the first volume of his *Lytton Strachey* (1967) that this further dimension of Keynes's life became common knowledge.

By then the intellectual and cultural climate was more forgiving to such disclosures. In Britain this was the era of a supposed consensus in economic policy: not simply agreement between the political parties, but an agreement to disagree within limits that each side thought of as Keynesian. 'It was an interesting mixture of planning and freedom, based on the economic teachings of Lord Keynes,' was the summary by the influential economic journalist Samuel Brittan in 1964.[17] Harold Macmillan, Conservative Prime Minister from 1957 to 1963, was proud to have been an early convert, as befitted his other role as the great man's publisher, with the *General Theory* a nice little earner on the Macmillan backlist.

In the United States, the election of John F. Kennedy in 1960 tested how much the new President had absorbed, twenty-three years previously at Harvard, when he took freshman economics in the year after the *General Theory* had arrived there. The chronicler of the Kennedy presidency, Arthur Schlesinger, with all the assurance of a fellow Harvard man, was to pronounce Kennedy 'unquestionably the first Keynesian President'.[18] Certainly the chairman of his Council of Economic Advisors, Walter Heller, was in this mould and was understandably proud that the President commented, after delivering a successful speech defending his tax cuts in late 1962: 'I gave them straight Keynes and Heller, and they loved it.'[19]

Many Republicans, however, remained to be won over. Though the Eisenhower years had seen massive investment in the American infrastructure, this was comfortably combined with the rhetoric of balanced budgets and ritual denunciations of government spending. The Democrats' inconsistency, especially after Vietnam plundered blood and treasure alike, was to run a war economy in denial about the costs of war. But the American boom of the mid-1960s finally adopted Keynes as a patron saint, presumably on the principle that you have to be safely dead to be canonised. Or perhaps it was a posthumous fulfilment of the time lag postulated in the last pages of the *General Theory*, where the famous claim that we may unwittingly become 'the slaves of some defunct economist' or 'academic scribbler' is explained by the fact that 'there are not many who are influenced by new theories after they are twenty-five or thirty years of age' so that ideas, when they triumph, 'are not likely to be the newest'.[20]

The cover story of *Time* magazine at the end of 1965 supplied the popular imprimatur: 'We Are All Keynesians Now.' The story, prominently and accessibly displayed, assured readers that ideas were powerful and that the world was indeed ruled by little else, just as Keynes had claimed thirty years previously. 'Now Keynes and his ideas, though they still make some people nervous, have been so widely accepted that they constitute both the new orthodoxy in the universities and the touchstone of economic management in Washington.' Not only was Heller's successor as chairman of the Council of Economic Advisors quoted to this effect, so was the economic adviser to Barry Goldwater, the defeated Republican presidential candidate in 1964. This was no less than Professor Milton Friedman of Chicago, 'the nation's leading conservative economist', and it was he who was credited with the headline phrase: 'We are all Keynesians now.'[21]

Here was a quotation in search of an author – like a lost dog wandering around, ready to lick any proffered hand. For Friedman was not anxious to claim it, and instead offered his gloss on what was evidently an off-the-cuff comment: 'In one sense, we are all Keynesians now; in another, nobody is any longer a Keynesian.'[22] So the friendless hound remained at loose for a few years before a potential owner was found, with a suitably impressive name to be inscribed on the dog-tag.

Thus the high-water mark for Keynes's political influence duly came when a Republican president was himself pressed into the assigned role. Richard Nixon had been in the White House for a couple of years when he outlined a budget for 1971–2 that responded to rising unemployment by planning a deficit as a stimulus for the US economy. He therefore took his message to the people. In the ABC television studios, where the President had been interviewed, he told one of the commentators afterwards that he was 'now a Keynesian in economics'.[23] Never renowned for a felicitous touch in politics, it was Nixon who was to be subsequently credited with the bastardised version – 'We are all Keynesians now' – which was to become the epitaph for an era.

No sooner had the hubristic words been pronounced than everything came unravelled. As the 1970s unfolded, the onset of economic troubles led to widespread questioning of whether Keynesianism had really provided a magic tool-kit for running the economy at full employment. The fiscal policies with which Keynes's name was posthumously associated, concentrating on government's ability to tax and spend, were now derided. Instead, monetary solutions were sought, focused on the supply of credit and interest rates. This was a very broad shift of priorities, both in analysis and in policy. One remarkable aspect of the controversy about these issues is how far the argument was personalised.

The name that came to rival that of Keynes was that of Milton Friedman. Indeed his own fame was to vary inversely with Keynes's reputation, which he therefore had a sort of perverse interest in sustaining, all the better to diminish it. If academic economists are asked to name Keynes's real intellectual rivals within their discipline in the twentieth century, they will often mention Schumpeter, with his vision of creative destruction, or Hayek, with his subtle intuitions about the wisdom of the market. It was Friedman who inherited the other role that Keynes had once occupied, as a publicist with an agenda steeped in prior ideological predilections. But whereas Keynes had exploited his public platform for polemical purposes long before he addressed 'my fellow economists' in the *General Theory*, Friedman trod a more conventional career path. He was the learned professor, who had published dense works on monetary policy. Only later, when the tide of opinion turned, did he establish a popular following and become an improbable media star as the front man of the 'Chicago School'.

The great landmark is generally supposed to be the speech that Friedman gave on monetary policy in Washington, DC, in December 1967. He gave it as his presidential address to the American Economic Association, so his professional credentials were already recognised. But the notion that Friedman laid down the operational principles of 'monetarism' on that occasion does not withstand perusal of what he actually said. In fact he spent almost all of his allotted time in warning what monetary policy could not do, and only in the last few minutes of his lecture did he talk about what it could do. His final advice was that the authorities should stop trying to manipulate employment levels and concentrate on some means of controlling the money supply. So we may now be surprised by the caution and circumspection with which Friedman developed his argument. But its object would have been clear enough to the listening professors: to 'undermine Keynes' key theoretical proposition, namely, that even in a world of flexible prices, a position of equilibrium at full employment might not exist'.[24]

Friedman was Keynes-through-the-looking-glass. Not only in theory but in practical policy options, they stood for opposites, and enjoyed equal and opposite swings of public favour. 'For years, the maverick views of Milton Friedman, the towering iconoclast of U.S. economics, attracted just about as much ridicule as respect,' reported *Time* magazine in 1969, at a time when Nixon was listening to the Chicago School, of which Friedman was now the acknowledged leader. 'Keynesian economics doesn't work,' Friedman forthrightly commented. 'But nothing is harder for men than to face facts that threaten to undermine strongly held beliefs.'[25] Keynes had voiced similar sentiments in his own day. And though Friedman had to endure Nixon's apostasy in the early 1970s, signs that the monetarists were winning the argument were indisputable by the time that Friedman was awarded the Nobel Prize for Economics in 1976.

In Britain the new political economy of Thatcherism had the doctrine of monetarism and the ethic of fiscal restraint at its heart. It was obviously a response to the combination of rising unemployment and rising inflation in the 1970s – a nightmare conjunction which self-professed Keynesians seemed unable to explain, still less remedy. In the British press, the turn against current Keynesianism could be seen in the widely read columns by Samuel Brittan of the *Financial Times* and Peter Jay of *The Times*. Denis Healey, Chancellor of the Exchequer in a Labour government, was exasperated by the mindset he found among his civil servants: 'In 1974 the Treasury was the slave of the greatest of all academic scribblers, Maynard Keynes himself.'[26] Likewise, in 1975, the financial commentator Tim Congdon expressed his frustration in an article in the magazine *Encounter*: 'In economics, the revered warrior in all confrontations is still John Maynard Keynes. A quote from Keynes, no matter how slight and trivial, appears to silence opposition.'[27]

No longer! Thatcher's closest advisers had the simple watchword: 'Keynes is dead.' 'At the macroeconomic level,' explained Nigel Lawson, soon to become Chancellor himself, 'our approach is what has come to be known as monetarism, in contradistinction to what has come to be known as Keynesianism, although the latter doctrine is a perversion of what Keynes actually preached himself.'[28] The targeting of the 'ism' rather than the man was significant.

Margaret Thatcher said the same, only louder. 'No, no, no,' she told one interviewer in 1979, 'I am afraid Keynesianism has gone mad and it wasn't in the least little bit what Keynes thought.'[29] Nor was this a stray remark – she returned happily to this theme on numerous occasions. In a speech to her party conference in 1984, explaining how the country had gone wrong after 1945, she notably abstained from imputing personal blame. 'Keynes had provided the diagnosis,' she said approvingly. 'It was all set out in the 1944 White Paper on Employment. I bought it then. I have it still.'[30] In case anyone challenged her to produce this relic, her famously capacious handbag stood ready. As she said on one occasion in the following year, 'I often quote Keynes, because Keynes is the most misquoted man.'[31] By contrast, in her years of power she avoided endorsing Friedman, possibly in the 1970s because his concept of a 'natural rate of employment' was politically combustible, probably in the 1980s because he offered criticisms of her government's monetarist strategy. 'Well, monetarist policy is far older than Mr Milton Friedman,' she brusquely told one interviewer in 1982, 'monetarist policy is as old as money…'[32]

Dead or not, Keynes would not lie down. His name appeared over 400 times in the *New York Times* during the 1970s, and the same during the 1980s, more than in either the 1950s or the 1960s. Even adversarial invocations of his name surely bestow some sort of compliment in an era that was not kind to his doctrines. Just as Thatcherism overthrew the Keynesian consensus in Britain, so the election of Ronald Reagan in 1980 brought a new economic regime to the USA.

To those who had become accustomed to a dichotomy between Keynesian and Friedmanite models, however, this was a baffling development. 'The rhetoric has been monetarist, but not the practice,' Friedman himself commented after the first two years.[33] One contrast with Thatcherism was that 'Reaganomics' showed itself more tolerant of budget deficits – just what British Keynesianism was accused of licensing in the bad old days, it might seem. The justifying theory was that a tax cut would pay for itself through creating an increase in government revenue. It would do so because the economic growth that would pay the taxes would be generated by the incentive of the tax cut itself. This benign cycle could indeed be given an oddly Keynesian twist. But it rested, of course, on blithe confidence in the response on the supply side. In practice government revenue did not make up the difference but led to persistent deficits.

Faith in the universal efficacy of the market became the big story, the master narrative. And historically high growth rates, sustained from the mid-1990s, inevitably fed a climate of complacency which had little time for the arguments that had dominated the previous half-century. Far from the market seeking stability within a framework provided by government, the terms of the argument were reversed. The market model increasingly became the template for government in an era of deregulation, outsourcing and privatisation. Government, in Reagan's epochal formula, was not the answer but was itself the problem.

It is unsurprising that, during the past thirty years, the name of Keynes has lost its gilt. True, it was still deployed by Gordon Brown, Labour's Chancellor of the Exchequer, in reproaching his Thatcherite predecessors at the Treasury. Lawson's mistake, according to Brown, was that 'having rejected the crude Keynesianism of the seventies he rejected Keynes's approach altogether when, instead, the real challenge was to interpret Keynes's important insights for the modern world'.[34]

Never wholly forgotten, Keynes was none the less marginalised. He was the man, too clever by half, who had peddled chimerical remedies that were simply not needed, so long as the economy was left to cure itself through the liberating impact of unrestrained market forces. His thinking was dismissed as 'depression economics', irrelevant in a world where depressions no longer happened.

And then came the great meltdown of 2008. Incomprehensibly, market forces, on which the rising generation had been taught to rely, failed to deliver the goods, failed to offer self-correction, failed to cope with a self-inflicted crisis of confidence. The media gave a perhaps simplistic view of what was hot and what was not. For about thirty years Keynes's reputation had languished; in about thirty days the defunct economist was rediscovered and rehabilitated. The British Chancellor of the Exchequer, Alistair Darling, was quick to declare on 19 October: 'Much of what Keynes wrote still makes sense.'[35] That week's issue of *Time* magazine decided to blow the dust off its cover story of 31 December 1965, 'We Are All Keynesians Now'. In exhuming the phrase, it exhumed Keynesianism itself and hardly needed to comment: 'Now it's coming back into fashion.'[36]

Keynes's roller-coaster reputation stands today at a critical moment which needs history as well as economics to be properly understood. There never was a timeless 'Keynes', whom we can demonise or mythologise at whim. Instead the historical Keynes inevitably found his current thinking influenced by the times in which he lived. He came up with ideas about immediate economic policy and also about the very foundations of theoretical economics. He has been often misunderstood, not only by his opponents but also by those who claimed to be his true adherents. The context of his own times and his own life is where we need to begin if we want to understand his continuing relevance and to make sense of John Maynard Keynes.

David Low, Solo Syndication / Associated Newspapers Ltd.

*The great cartoonist David Low, an admirer of
Keynes, captures him in repose in 1931.*

I

'A religion and no morals'
John Maynard Keynes, 1883–1924

H E   W A S   B O R N in the same year that Karl Marx died. His father, John Neville Keynes, was always known by his middle name, perhaps because his own father was also called John (long a favourite name in the family). A shrewd and energetic widower, with a thriving horticultural and business career in Salisbury, John Keynes in 1851 had taken, as his second wife, a farmer's daughter called Anna Maynard Neville. Hence her son, John Neville Keynes, born the next year, was known by his mother's maiden name and his own eldest son, John Maynard Keynes, was given his grandmother's middle name following his birth on 5 June 1883. Though in his published works he styled himself J. M. Keynes, as was conventional at that time, it was as Maynard that he was known to family and friends.

Neville Keynes went to the University of Cambridge, which was a big step for him. And he stayed there, which was of formative significance for his children. Neville was interested in logic and political economy, and thus had the makings of a career in economics at just the time that this was emerging as an academic discipline. He was once offered a post at the University of Chicago but wrote back that he was 'far too rooted in Cambridge'.[1] Perhaps young Maynard might otherwise have been brought up as an economist of the Chicago School.

Neville Keynes was a man for whom roots were very important. His family had been Baptists; that of his wife Florence Ada Brown, whom he had married a year before Maynard's birth, were Congregationalists. They did not need to be regular chapel-goers themselves to remain aware of their heritage in a tradition of religious Dissent that stretched back to Oliver Cromwell (a Cambridge undergraduate, of course). They were axiomatically Liberals in politics. It was naturally a Liberal government that had broken the Anglican monopoly on the ancient universities – applying, in a sense, free trade principles in religion and education.

Florence was twenty-two when Maynard was born and remained an active influence upon him until his death – she was to outlive her son by twelve years. She was a pioneer in civic life in stuffy, male-dominated Cambridge and became the city's first woman councillor, alderman and mayor. Her career paralleled Neville's rise in the administrative structure of the modern university that was slowly emerging from its monastic shell. Town and gown came together in their household; Maynard later donated the city's Arts Theatre as a tribute to his parents. When, after the publication of *The Economic Consequences of the Peace*, the press cuttings started to pile up, Florence began keeping the scrapbooks that chronicled her talented elder son's career. Maynard's younger sister Margaret later emulated her mother in espousing progressive causes in local government; her husband, A. V. Hill, was a physiologist who won the Nobel Prize in 1922. Their younger brother, later Sir Geoffrey Keynes, became an eminent surgeon and bibliographer, who married Margaret Elizabeth Darwin, granddaughter of Charles Darwin (naturally another Cambridge man). The Keynes family became part of a Cambridge elite where everybody knew everybody.

Maynard had a privileged upbringing. But this was not at all the world of the ancestral, Anglican, titled, landed British upper classes but an offshoot of an intellectual aristocracy with different roots. Florence and Neville had high-minded, plain-living friends among the first generation of dons who were permitted to marry and live outside their colleges. The Keyneses were to spend sixty-seven years of married life in a newly built house near the station, at 6 Harvey Road, its William Morris wallpaper gracing the walls of the dining room to the end. Throughout most of six decades, whenever he could, Maynard went there for Sunday lunch, when his father liked to open a good claret.

It was Roy Harrod's biography that put into circulation the phrase 'the presuppositions of Harvey Road'. It has become an influential piece of shorthand for the assumptions about British society on which young Maynard was brought up. 'Reforms would be within a framework of stable and unquestioned social values,' Harrod explained, taking for granted 'the security and good order of the British Empire'. A crucial presupposition was 'the idea that the government of Britain was and would continue to be in the hands of an intellectual aristocracy using the methods of persuasion'.[2] Though the notion has often been taken too literally, which is a tribute to Harrod's eloquence, there is real insight here. Keynes's temperament may have been iconoclastic; he may sometimes have been carried away by his own ingenuity in putting the case against the conventional wisdom; but he retained a lifelong commitment to the strategy of institutional reform through reasoned argument.

Young Maynard's sheer cleverness was soon recognised by his parents. They sent him to the best private schools: first in Cambridge, then to Eton College, where he won a scholarship. The scholarship was more significant as a sign of intellectual distinction than as a means of paying the bills at the most prestigious school in the country. From Eton it was a natural progression back to Cambridge. He did not, however, apply to his father's college, Pembroke, but to King's College, which was of similar antiquity to Eton, both founded by King Henry VI. King's College Chapel, standing perpendicular to the River Cam, is among the architectural wonders of Britain, its aesthetic appeal complemented by the engineering marvel of its high-vaulted stone ceiling. Maynard loved it, though not for the religion. He marvelled at its capacious sense of space, tentatively suggesting on one later occasion, when he was college bursar, that it might be the solution to his over-speculation in grain futures, now requiring storage.

Like his father, then, Maynard was to make his career in Cambridge and to become an economist. All this was given to him on a plate. It seems in many ways a narrow career path, almost predestined; but it was not altogether straightforward.

It was one of Ronald Reagan's bemused discoveries as president that this man Keynes, of whom he heard so much, did not even have a degree in economics. True enough, at Cambridge Keynes read mathematics, the university's forte since the time of Isaac Newton. He duly sat for the tripos (as the BA degree examinations are called in Cambridge) with its traditional way of ranking those candidates excelling in mathematics – he was Twelfth Wrangler in 1905. This was a good result, in its way, equivalent to first-class honours in other subjects, putting him well into the top 10 per cent of candidates; but it meant that eleven mathematicians in the university had done better.

Only later that year, having already graduated, did he begin his study of economics. A separate tripos in the subject had been established only a couple of years previously, largely through the efforts of Professor Alfred Marshall, the doyen of the profession, whose authoritative work *Principles of Economics* (1890) went through edition after edition. And, inevitably, Marshall was a family friend, ready to agree to teach the Keynes boy himself. It was the usual Cambridge system of individual supervision, one hour a week for the eight weeks of the teaching term – the only formal instruction in economics that Keynes ever received. But he impressed Marshall, who wrote on one of his essays: 'I trust that your future career may be one in which you will not cease to be an economist.'[3]

True enough, he did not cease. But Marshall's rather odd phrasing has a point. For Keynes never settled for simply becoming an economist in a rigorous professional or academic sense. He took pride in the fact that in Cambridge, economics had grown out of the moral sciences tripos, rooted in philosophy. The economist, he wrote later, 'must be mathematician, historian, statesman, philosopher' and 'must understand symbols and speak in words'. It was this combination of gifts that made good economists such rare birds. 'An easy subject, at which very few excel!'[4]

Also, he was too easily distracted to focus on simply becoming an economist. In career terms, his big idea in 1906 was to enter the Civil Service through the competitive examinations held annually, with a range of subjects examined. In these national examinations, held in London, Keynes came first overall in logic, psychology, English essay and political science; second in moral and metaphysical philosophy. What enraged him was his run of marks elsewhere. 'Really knowledge seems an absolute bar to success,' he expostulated. 'I have done worst in the only two subjects of which I possess a solid knowledge – Mathematics and Economics.'[5] As a result, he came second overall: to a brilliant candidate from Oxford, Otto Niemeyer, who thus had first choice of which government department he would enter. Niemeyer naturally picked the Treasury, in which he rose to become a top civil servant in the 1920s, defending Treasury orthodoxy with dogged relish against the early assaults of the Cambridge economist whom he had bested twenty years previously.

Beaten to the prized Treasury post, Keynes chose the India Office. Here in Whitehall, the seat of executive government, though junior in rank, Keynes led the life of a civil servant of the administrative class, selected as a mandarin, groomed to run the Empire. He was always against both late nights and early mornings, saying, 'I snuff the candle at both ends.'[6] So the gentlemanly eleven-to-five days at the India Office passed equably, though leaving him with little sense of fulfilment.

Keynes acquired, almost in spite of himself, an expertise that later served him well. His first published book, *Indian Currency and Finance* (1913), was a product of his official responsibilities, which forced him to master the intricacies of how India's historic Silver Standard had been affected by the imposition, under the British Raj, of an international Gold Standard. In the USA such issues had been to the fore in the bimetallist campaigns of the 1890s, when William Jennings Bryan had declaimed that 'you shall not crucify mankind upon a cross of gold'.[7] In Britain, the ripples of the bimetallic debate were smaller; they had come and gone; few found such questions at all interesting. Until the First World War caused its suspension, the Gold Standard was largely taken for granted – especially by those who did not really understand it. But Keynes had already been introduced to a case study in its potentially perverse effects. This was to affect his views on policy in the 1920s.

In career terms, too, the India Office seemed silver to the Treasury's gold. Keynes's door into the Treasury had been blocked by Niemeyer, and stayed blocked for the moment. But his duties left him ample time to pursue his intellectual interests. He began to prepare a dissertation, to be submitted for a Fellowship at King's. In Cambridge, becoming a college Fellow, or don, was in those days the route to what we would now call a tenure-track academic appointment.

Keynes was unsuccessful in the Fellowship competition the first time around in 1908. But his chances improved when, after twenty-one months at the India Office, he resigned to take up an opportunity of returning to Cambridge, in effect as Marshall's teaching assistant, paid out of Marshall's own pocket. It might lead to a Fellowship; it might lead to nothing. Keynes took the chance. It came off. In 1909 he was elected to a Fellowship, which he was to hold until his death. Indeed he treasured the connection with King's to the extent of later serving as bursar, responsible for the college's finances, for the last twenty-two years of his life – even when weighed down with heavy commitments, in London and Washington alike, during the Second World War.

In Cambridge, Keynes was at home, in every sense. He now thought that he had a real job. 'The work of a don is the hardest work in the world,' he assured one of his London friends, adding: 'I am becoming little more than a machine for selling economics by the hour.'[8] But still he did not settle down to the sort of work that was in the mainstream of economics. Instead, his chief energies went into preparing a revised version of his Fellowship dissertation for publication. This was delayed by other commitments, notably his short Indian currency book, a by-product of the India Office connection. But by August 1914 most of the bulky, academic volume on which he had lavished his intermittent scholarly labours was set up in type. This could hardly have been done at a worse moment. It became a war casualty and was not finally published for a further seven years, after *The Economic Consequences of the Peace* had already given its author name recognition among the reading public.

For readers expecting an equally lively sequel to that bestseller, *A Treatise on Probability* (1921), running to over 500 pages, would have come as a disappointment. It certainly did not fit the public image that Keynes the publicist had suddenly acquired. Nor did it look to economists like a proper fulfilment of his professional duties. They generally ignored the book, not just at the time but for most of the next sixty years.

Even when the *General Theory* provided fertile hints about the importance of probability and uncertainty in unsettling our notions about decision-making, the leads were largely neglected. Yet they cry out for attention if we are to see the full point of Keynes's thinking. In the long perspective of history, we can remedy such neglect. We can now see how the impact of Keynesianism took particular forms that were specific to their own time and place, but are not necessarily relevant to us today. Conversely, the thinking of the historical Keynes still has a surprising capacity to enlighten us.

Keynes's early life has been the subject of a great deal of disinformation. One reason for this is already apparent: that his homosexuality had to be covered up. Another reason, however, is that he himself laid a false trail in his brilliant memoir, 'My Early Beliefs'. This was not written for publication but for an audience of his old friends in 1938, reflecting on their common experience. In it Keynes claimed that they 'repudiated entirely customary morals, conventions and traditional wisdom'.[9] It is a short step from these provocative remarks to the conclusion – all too readily drawn, and not only by critics – that the young Keynes lacked any sense of social responsibility, showed damaging political naivety and was consumed with an arrogant narcissism.

He was indeed a practising homosexual for perhaps twenty years. Among his papers there survives a list of his partners, year by year from 1901 to 1915, comprising mainly his own friends but also some casual pick-ups: 'Stable boy of Park Lane'; 'Auburn haired of Marble Arch'; 'Lift boy of Vauxhall'; 'Jew boy'.[10] In Britain homosexual activity had been criminalised in the late Victorian era, and the trial and imprisonment of Oscar Wilde were a great public scandal during Maynard's teenage years at Eton. The scandal may now seem to lie in the fact that Wilde was persecuted in this way. But not until the liberal reforms of the 1960s were the statutory penalties removed and only in the late twentieth century were 'gay rights' established in British as in North American society. Keynes would not have understood this terminology. He lived in an era when a gay night out simply meant that the wit flowed like champagne (and vice versa). But when his circle talked for effect of 'the higher sodomy', they left themselves equally likely to be misunderstood by later generations. That, of course, is a difficulty that Harrod's official biography of Keynes circumvented by giving a deliberately misleading impression of the private life of his hero.

Keynes's schooldays were spent at Eton (boys only) and his undergraduate career at King's (bigger boys). At Cambridge there were only two colleges for women in a university that was not to grant them full graduate status until after the Second World War. Among the nineteen male colleges, King's was long regarded as peculiar in tolerating, even fostering, open displays of both affection and affectation between its members, in a manner that we now call camp. If young Maynard's sexuality was somewhat ill-defined, he could hardly have been put in a better place to cross the line from homosocial display to homosexual activity. Later, when he risked cruising the London streets for casual sex, he courted real dangers. But in Cambridge the long arm of the law did not meddle into what went on between the young gentlemen, living cheek by jowl in their college rooms.

For Keynes and his friends, class privilege and sexual liberation walked hand in hand. It was in his student days at Cambridge, and then in his Civil Service interlude in London, that Keynes's sexual impulses were channelled into a series of passionate friendships with other young men, many of them already more sexually experienced than himself. They got a thrill from using a more overt, explicit, shocking language than their actual sexual deeds probably warranted at the time.

Most of his friends were either in King's or at Trinity College, the biggest and richest college in the university. The key figure here was Giles Lytton Strachey – like Maynard, he was known by his middle name. The Stracheys were an upper-middle-class family with strong administrative and military links to the British Raj – a stiff-upper-lip tradition of which the camp figure of Lytton was a walking, talking repudiation. He preferred talking, in his fluting voice, to walking, of course. Maynard was later to transfer his affections to the dashing young painter Duncan Grant, Lytton's cousin in the extended Strachey family.

The young Virginia Stephen, whose own family had a similar background and ethos to the Stracheys, later liked to dub her forebears, with feminist disdain, 'the men who ruled India'. It did not escape her that they were all men, nor that only the young men of such families were routinely packed off for an expensive education in Cambridge – like her own adored elder brother Thoby (who died tragically young of typhoid). Virginia was to meet Thoby's exciting friends in due course: Lytton Strachey, so outrageous that he even once proposed marriage to her; E. M. Forster (Morgan to his friends), a quiet man whose first novel, *Where Angels Fear to Tread*, had not yet been published; Clive Bell, an aesthete who subsequently married her sister Vanessa; Leonard Woolf, who went out to rule part of Ceylon (temporarily) – and whose proposal Virginia finally did accept, thus acquiring the surname under which her own writings achieved worldwide fame.

Virginia Woolf's first contact with Maynard Keynes, then, was through this close-knit circle of Cambridge friends, who were so wrapped up in each other and in their common membership of a society called the Apostles. The Apostles, founded in 1820 as the Cambridge Conversazione Society, had developed a strong sense of corporate identity and secrecy. They were a self-selected group of male undergraduates, but their meetings on Saturday evenings were attended also by some older men, mainly dons, who retained life membership. They would meet to hear and discuss a paper given by one of their number. It was an intellectual rather than an academic forum, more a gathering of intimate friends than a seminar.

Out of this grew 'Bloomsbury' – not really a group, certainly not a formally organised one. The name was simply that of the then unfashionable district of London south of Euston Station, with the town houses round its elegant squares shabby and dilapidated at this time. It was not only cheaper to live there than in respectable Kensington but also less constraining for adventurous young people. In 1905 the four-storey house at 46 Gordon Square was tenanted by the younger Stephens – Thoby and his brother Adrian, and their sisters Virginia and Vanessa – and became the seedbed of what they simply called 'Bloomsbury', identified as the network of like-minded friends, originally a dozen or so, who eventually became an iconic cultural landmark. Their Thursday evening 'At Homes' testified to their own Apostolic succession. They were shockingly frank, or frankly shocking, in discussing all manner of things that interest young people, especially sex, and in front of women too.

Keynes attended frequently, especially when he was at the India Office, escaping for the evening from his small apartment near Whitehall. Moreover, after returning to Cambridge to become a don, he maintained a *pied-à-terre* in Bloomsbury from 1909. He found rooms in a house in Fitzroy Square for a couple of years. Just a few doors away was the house taken by Virginia and Adrian Stephen, while the newly wed Clive and Vanessa Bell remained in Gordon Square. Maynard later shared a house with Virginia and Adrian in nearby Brunswick Square, on a collective basis. This was thought perilously unconventional by Virginia's protective friends, since she had on the premises not only Maynard and Duncan Grant but the heterosexual Leonard Woolf too – they were to marry shortly. After quitting Brunswick Square, Maynard occupied rooms at a couple of other short-lived addresses in Bloomsbury before, in 1916, he took over from Clive and Vanessa Bell the lease of 46 Gordon Square, the same house where his friends had first come together eleven years previously.

No. 46 Gordon Square, truly the hub of their Bloomsbury, was to remain his London home for the rest of his life.

Bloomsbury, in this sense, began as a transplant. It transported to London much of the rebellious ethos of the Strachey–Stephen clique among the Apostles, while reinforcing its membership with similarly talented women, among whom Virginia Woolf became pre-eminent. Many of Keynes's friends were homosexual, but few were misogynists. Many were active supporters of woman suffrage. Bloomsbury was justly accused of being a mutual admiration society. Its members developed a strong sense of their own identity and a pride in their own diverse achievements as the years went by. One manifestation of this was their 'memoir club', at which they took turns to read papers to each other, licensed in tone by long friendship, confident that the in-jokes would be understood, and ready to say to each other things that outsiders might well misconstrue.

It was to a meeting of the memoir club in 1938, as the Munich crisis brewed, that Keynes read 'My Early Beliefs'. Under the cloud of a threatened war, he gave an evocative account of a lost age of innocence, his paper contrived for effects that it duly evoked. 'The beauty and unworldliness of it' struck Virginia Woolf as she listened in the dusk, and she wrote in her diary that it made 'a very human satisfactory meeting'.[11]

Keynes was talking in layman's terms – but about complex and intractable issues. These initially seem baffling to many readers who suddenly find that they are confronting intellectual problems that threaten to spoil their light-hearted relish for overhearing Bloomsbury gossip with just half an ear open. But there is a time bomb ticking here which helps us understand the later explosive effect of Keynes's thinking.

'My Early Beliefs' speaks of the influence of the Cambridge philosopher Professor G. E. Moore upon the impressionable young men who sat at his feet. Keynes here makes a distinction between private ethics, which he calls 'religion', and public duty, which he calls 'morals'. And he makes the provocative claim that young Apostles like himself had 'a religion and no morals'.[12] Self-absorbed in personal dilemmas – so 'My Early Beliefs' suggests – they had no appreciation of the wicked world outside, and no reason to concern themselves with its problems. Such was Keynes's confession before his friends.

But was it a true confession? Influential accounts of Keynes's life have accepted it more or less at face value, thus arguing that there was a chasm in his thinking. We need to establish whether it is in fact true that the young Keynes found no intellectual bridge between our personal ethical obligations and our political responsibilities to the community. It is impossible to give an adequate answer to this question without becoming rather technical – much more so than the artistic rendering in 'My Early Beliefs'. But it is worth the effort because otherwise we are left with a misleading caricature.

We need to go back for a moment to the years of work and thought that Keynes put into his *Treatise on Probability*. We see a very clever young man at full stretch in grappling with intensely close-textured academic issues. The nub of the issue, however, is both clear and important. The gist of Keynes's argument is that probability cannot simply be measured by observed frequency. It is no good counting how many times a coin actually comes down heads or tails in order to determine the probabilities, in advance, of any single toss – the chances are always fifty-fifty.

Keynes's theory of probability thus depends on expectations, not on actual outcomes. It does not, however, collapse into a purely subjective view. Though rejecting actual frequency as the objective test, he seeks to be objective in the assessment of prior probabilities. It is an assessment that necessarily has to be made in advance, weighing one probability against another, without any absolute assurance as to the outcome. So this is a probabilistic view of ethics, judging actions by likely consequences. Keynes argued that it made no sense to say that we must know *for certain* what the outcome will be before we are entitled to exercise our discretion.

Whoever would have supposed otherwise? All the Apostles knew the answer to that question. For their revered Professor Moore maintained exactly this: that we should not presume to challenge any general rule without certain knowledge of the consequences.

Keynes's conflicting view acknowledges the social utility of rules and conventions ('morals'). The nub of his own argument is that, none the less, it can be justifiable for an individual to break the rules (becoming an 'immoralist' in this provocative vocabulary) if this is judged the most *likely* way to produce a better outcome. And that judgement will necessarily have to be exercised on the basis of expectations.

After all, in real life, which we live forwards, necessarily ignorant of the future, the consequences that seem probable to us *in advance* – what we reasonably expect to happen – are all that we have to go on in decision-making. But it is still justifiable to exercise our discretion, even under these conditions. And we do so, not on a hedonistic whim, but as responsible citizens, fulfilling a moral duty.

This is a sophisticated position, with lifelong implications for Keynes's thinking. As we shall see in Chapter 4, it underpins what the *General Theory* tells us about probability and uncertainty, and about the need to act under conditions of uncertainty. And the essence of it is in the *Treatise on Probability*.

Yet that is not how Keynes chose to decode these admittedly difficult issues for his friends in the memoir club. Instead, he put forward the provocative taunt: 'We were, that is to say, in the strict sense of the term, immoralists.'[13] This was too much for some of his hearers. Leonard Woolf – who had vetted Keynes as an undergraduate for membership of the Apostles and who remained active alongside him in all the usual good causes of the liberal left

– could see the danger signal flashing, at least once he read his old friend's teasing memoir in cold print, after its posthumous publication in 1948.

It was the earnest, high-minded Woolf who straightforwardly protested later that 'we were not "immoralists"', using the term in the ordinary rather than the 'strict sense'.[14] He realised that many outside their charmed circle were liable to be misled about the moral compass of the Apostles and Bloomsbury alike. By calling anyone who made a principled decision to defy any general convention an 'immoralist', Keynes had been too clever by half.

Keynes was a political animal, to an extent that has rarely been given its due. The big Bloomsbury biographies that have flourished during recent decades have illuminated many passages in his life but have generally played down the politics. Yet Keynes's earliest biographers, the younger friends who actually knew the man, did not make this mistake. Before the First World War, according to Sir Austin Robinson's long obituary notice of his revered colleague in the *Economic Journal* in 1947, 'Keynes' absorbing interest at this stage of his life was politics'. Of course it was clearly on record that he had been president of the University Liberal Club and was also elected president of the Cambridge Union Society, the main student debating forum. What Robinson meant by Keynes's absorbing concern for politics can be sensed from his further comment that 'beneath a Georgian skin there peeped out from time to time an almost Victorian sense of moral purpose and obligation; neither Eton, nor Cambridge, nor Bloomsbury had obliterated wholly his heritage from generations of Keyneses and Browns'.[15] Harrod, who likewise knew Keynes personally from the early 1920s, conveyed some of this sense of ethical commitment to reform in writing of 'the presuppositions of Harvey Road'.

It was natural that young Maynard should have identified with the Liberal Party, like his parents before him. The great Liberal electoral landslide of 1906 came at the end of his student days in Cambridge. It was one of those rare political moments that generate widespread hopes of change. After nearly twenty years of Conservative government, a Liberal government was established which, with support from the new Labour Party, dominated British politics until the Great War.

Partly this was a negative reaction to the tariff proposals that the Conservatives now put forward, promising that 'Tariff Reform Means Work For All'. This aim might sound distinctly radical, rather like an anticipation of a Keynesian full-employment policy. But young Maynard remained, in fiscal policy at least, a small-c conservative, clinging to the good old doctrine of Free Trade, with capital letters: an article of faith on which Liberals and Labour were united. Indeed, as an orthodox economist, schooled by the great Marshall, he became a useful platform speaker, trotting out arguments on behalf of Free Trade that had seemed axiomatically true ever since Adam Smith founded the profession of economics upon the concept of the division of labour. Keynes thus spoke, as he later admitted in the *General Theory*, 'as a faithful pupil of the classical school who did not at that time doubt what he had been taught and entertained on this matter no reserves at all'.[16]

The government that Herbert Henry Asquith led from 1908, in which the dynamic David Lloyd George became Chancellor of the Exchequer, made a more positive appeal to Keynes's progressive instincts. Its reform agenda – old-age pensions, German-style health insurance, experimental unemployment insurance – marked a break with the old Liberalism of laissez-faire in domestic policy. This New Liberalism was plainly congenial to Keynes, intellectually and temperamentally, serving to enlist his ancestral political prejudices behind an agenda that had a strong social and economic bent. But not until the 1920s did he himself develop such themes, especially in regard to unemployment, in hands-on political activity.

When Britain went to war against Germany in 1914 the Liberal Party found itself enmeshed in an ongoing crisis that sapped its power and confidence alike. Asquith, who had won all the prizes at Oxford and at the Bar, calm and magisterial, was a master at keeping his Cabinet united by adroit compromises. But many Liberals came to feel, as the war dragged on, that their own principles were being compromised in the process. Certainly many of Keynes's Bloomsbury friends felt that war was simply the wrong way of settling international issues. This led some, like Duncan Grant, Keynes's former lover, to object to military service. It led others, like Leonard Woolf, to think in terms of a redemptive postwar settlement, with some scheme of international government. Keynes had sympathy with both positions and, above all, with those who held them.

Meanwhile he fulfilled one of his own great ambitions: to be accepted into the Treasury. Keynes served as a temporary wartime civil servant and took to the administrative life like a duck to water. Everyone in his grade seemed to have a good degree in classics or mathematics from the elite universities – like his friend Ralph Hawtrey, Nineteenth Wrangler in 1901, whom he had known as an Apostle at Cambridge; or his nemesis in the 1906 competition, Otto Niemeyer, a first in Greats at Oxford; or other 'first class clerks' (as they were called) with whom Keynes would continue arguing for the next twenty years.

Keynes relished the fact that the Treasury was 'an institution which came to possess attributes of institutions like a college or a City company, or the Church of England'. He loved its atmosphere: 'very clever, very dry and in a certain sense very cynical; intellectually self-confident and not subject to the whims of people who feel that they are less hidden, and are not quite sure that they know their case'. He later confessed to becoming 'Treasury-minded' and lauded the unique authority that the Treasury exercised within the British structure of government – comparing it (in 1921) with Washington, DC, where 'the Treasury has very little authority beyond looking after the collection of taxes'.[17] How much better to be in Whitehall, where the clever official who won an argument could pull the levers of power! Since the British Treasury worked closely with the Bank of England, as 'the authorities', they really governed the workings of the whole financial system.

Keynes had already been consulted, at the outbreak of war, about banking policy and interest rates. His expertise was recognised quickly in the Treasury, where he was given a range of tasks that show how much his skills were valued. Increasingly he became responsible for the external finance of the war, monitoring loans from the United States and fathoming the complexities of the flows of funds between the Allies. It was a system in which Britain's financial strength turned out to be a mixed blessing, since British credit was used to raise US dollars that were then channelled to less credit-worthy Allies, leaving Britain with outstanding liabilities in the United States. Keynes's mind was becoming focused on the effects of such transfers across the exchanges in a way that highlighted – suggestively for his own future interests – what we might call the economic consequences of the war.

Keynes was certainly prepared to support the war effort in this way. The Treasury was a small department, but extremely well connected, and with a finger in every pie. And it was thrilling to meet the great men of the day. He started to be invited by the Asquiths to 10 Downing Street, to play bridge. This simultaneously satisfied Keynes's appetite for gambling and, so his Bloomsbury friends implied, social climbing too. When he was part of a country house party along with the Prime Minister, so the story goes, they were announced as 'Mr Keynes and another gentleman'.[18] He was firmly in the Asquith camp, and accordingly ready to question the logic with which Lloyd George, having left the Treasury for the Ministry of Munitions in 1915, urged a bigger, bolder mobilisation of men and *matériel* alike.

Hence the potency of the issue of conscription for military service. The British tradition was that of a professional army plus voluntary enlistment in wartime. How, then, to enlist an army of millions to man the trenches? Keynes's advice to the new Chancellor, the Asquithian Reginald McKenna, that conscription was unnecessary since Britain's financial strength would be better deployed in other ways, was mounted as an economic argument, and of a highly orthodox kind at that. It was surely driven by an underlying passion against the very notion of conscription. Among Keynes's friends, Lytton Strachey and the brilliant philosopher Bertrand Russell were not alone in their forthright and prominent opposition to compulsory military service. Russell was to lose his lectureship at Trinity College, Cambridge. The stakes were high, personally as well as politically or militarily.

By the end of 1915, Asquith realised that the issue could be put off no longer. The admission of Conservative ministers to a coalition government the previous May had strengthened the voices in favour of conscription, and when the growing impatience of Lloyd George prompted his conversion later that year, Asquith judged that it was time to implement an adroit settlement. The new legislation was passed by the House of Commons in January 1916, opposed by three-quarters of the Irish Nationalist Party, who were joined by a few dozen Liberal and Labour MPs still unreconciled to this surrender of their libertarian, voluntarist principles. Asquith remained Prime Minister; McKenna did not resign; nor did Keynes, though pressed to do so by both Strachey and Russell.

The law now required single men to attest their willingness to serve in the armed forces. Keynes was plainly in a dilemma. Personally he had exemption from military service so long as he was required in the Treasury; and the government service would hardly agree to release an able official who was proving himself indispensable. In this sense, the issue did not arise. Keynes simply had no need to lodge an official objection to being required to serve. But this is just what he did on 28 February 1916, three days before the deadline. Again, this is something that Harrod covered up.

The document that Keynes submitted survives in his papers. It shows that he did not object in principle to offering himself for military service, but reserved his own right to decide. 'I am not prepared on such an issue as this to surrender my right of decision, as to what is or is not my duty, to any other person, and I should think it morally wrong to do so.'[19] This was a perfect example of his argument, as an 'immoralist', that one had the right to decide such matters oneself. Lytton Strachey's position on conscription differed in that he ruled out aiding the war in any way. And when Strachey was called to appear in person, the theatricality was much enhanced, especially when he was challenged as to what he would do if he saw a German soldier attempting to rape his sister. 'I should try and come between them,' his biographer records the answer. But this account also recorded that Strachey, taxed with objecting to all wars, responded in his piercing voice: 'Oh no, not at all. Only this one.'[20] Like Keynes, his principle was that he reserved his own discretion. Again, it was somewhat academic, since Strachey was plainly physically unfit to serve in any case.

The maxim that reason is the slave of the passions is often worth remembering when examining Keynes's utterances. On conscription, his argument had a clear intellectual consistency. Whether he would have felt the need to produce such a reason, at such a moment, but for the passions of his friends is another matter. They did not fail to observe that Maynard seemed to be having it both ways. When asked to attend in person to justify his conscientious objection, Keynes could grandly reply that he was too busy with Treasury business. The authorities were totally unimpressed; common sense told the bureaucrats pushing the papers that this Mr Keynes had exemption anyway; there was simply no point in pursuing the matter; the file was closed.

Keynes thus served out the war in the safety of the Treasury. Lloyd George displaced Asquith as Prime Minister in December 1916, in a coalition with the Conservatives that was to survive the war itself. Keynes naturally sided with the remnant of Asquithian exiles. Their position left them closer to the Labour Party than to the Conservatives, especially in foreign policy. Leonard Woolf was to serve as secretary of Labour's new Advisory Committees on International Questions, propagating his ideas about a league of nations. Bloomsbury was happy to follow the crowd in finding a hero in President Woodrow Wilson, who had brought the United States into the war in 1917, evoking a vision of a magnanimous peace and some kind of league to maintain it.

When an armistice was eventually agreed (or imposed) in November 1918, Keynes was soon caught up in the arguments about making Germany pay for the war. Lloyd George called a snap election so as to cash in on his reputation as the man who won the war, to ratify his own leadership of the coalition and to give himself a mandate to negotiate peace terms. The rough and tumble of electioneering did not nurture a Wilsonian approach in Britain (nor in the United States). One of Lloyd George's ministers, Sir Eric Geddes, found his moment of fame through a pungent remark about how to treat Germany. 'We will get out of her all you can squeeze out of a lemon and a bit more,' he said. 'I will squeeze her until you can hear the pips squeak.' Keynes was to give this quotation worldwide currency in *The Economic Consequences of the Peace*.[21] He was enabled to do so because the speech had been given in the Guildhall at Cambridge and Florence Keynes had, as usual, saved and filed the newspaper clipping.

Lloyd George won a great election victory in December 1918. His coalition supporters now filled the House of Commons. One of them, the future Conservative leader Stanley Baldwin, was a Treasury minister, in the office next to that of Keynes, who asked him what the new members looked like. 'A lot of hard-faced men who look as if they had done well out of the war,' said Baldwin – another quotation that was to become famous through Keynes's book.'[22]

None of this boded well for the Paris peace conference. Lloyd George went there as one of the Big Four, alongside Clemenceau of France, Orlando of Italy and, much the biggest, Wilson of the United States, who also had the biggest delegation, of 1,200 officials. The British sent 200, Keynes among them. He was head of a small staff responsible for a range of economic decisions, much over-burdened and working hours that would have appalled the pre-war India Office: 8.30 a.m. to midnight for weeks on end. One of his top concerns was the provision of food supplies to impoverished Germany, which plainly needed more than squeezed lemons to sustain it. But the reparations demanded from Germany, for the damages of a war it was blamed for starting, came to occupy top place on his agenda.

Keynes's own idea had been simple: to cancel war debts and start from there. This would have left Britain more or less where it was, forgoing what it was notionally owed by its indigent Allies but escaping its own huge liabilities to the United States. Naturally the American view was different. So the costs of the war, direct or indirect, had to be assessed. If only the direct costs of military devastation were counted, maybe Germany could realistically afford to pay – overwhelmingly to France, of course. But the claims of the British Empire, though indirect, were hardly likely to be overlooked by Lloyd George; and if he nodded, the combative Australian Prime Minister, William Hughes, was there to wake him up and stir him up. Thus the logic was to demand that Germany be faced with the full costs of the war, apportioning the gains between the victorious Allies.

Keynes did not have clean hands. He was implicated in the day-to-day, night-by-night haggling over the scale of reparations more closely than his subsequent protests might indicate, leaving some liberal Americans scornful. He was no political innocent. Perhaps he had become caught up in the sort of stratagems, 'by devious paths', characteristic of Lloyd George's statecraft: 'that this is the best of which a democracy is capable – to be jockeyed, humbugged, cajoled along the right road.' Keynes wrote as an insider, or at least an ex-insider, when he reflected: 'A preference for truth or for sincerity *as a method* may be a prejudice based on some aesthetic or personal standard, inconsistent, in politics, with practical good.'[23] At any rate, captivated by his own adroitness, he overestimated his personal ability to influence the final postwar settlement from inside – a mistake he was to make again at the end of the Second World War.

In the event, Keynes watched the inexorable process unfolding in Paris, largely powerless to mitigate what he saw as its evil effects. He decided to resign, planning a sort of phased retreat from Paris. When he first wrote this to his mother, she replied: 'How I wish I could run over to you & take you under my wing & protect you from the wicked world as I should do in a physical illness.'[24] He resisted pleas to reconsider his resignation from the Chancellor of the Exchequer, the Conservative Austen Chamberlain, with whom he got on well. 'The Prime Minister is leading us all into a morass of destruction,' Keynes told Chamberlain.[25] In June 1919, three weeks before the treaty was signed, Keynes left Paris. He went straight home to Cambridge.

By the end of July he had got an offer to publish *The Economic Consequences of the Peace*. His publisher was his Eton schoolfriend Daniel Macmillan, brother of Harold, the future Prime Minister. Because Daniel Macmillan was away at a crucial moment, Keynes varied the terms, in effect assuming the risk himself either way. So if the book had failed, he stood to lose his own money, but when it succeeded, the author rather than the publisher netted the bulk of the profits. Little wonder that Keynes subsequently kept to this arrangement for other books.

The Economic Consequences of the Peace was meant to be 40,000 words; it grew to 60,000 (this book is about the same). Keynes kept at it steadily and by October, when he had to return to his academic duties in Cambridge, drafts were ready for perusal. Asquith advised him to omit the portrait of Lloyd George, which he did, and his mother advised likewise on his references to Wilson – unavailingly. By the end of 1919, with heroic work by the publishers, the book was out and Keynes was thereby transported from obscurity into the public forum. The final sentence on the last page reads: 'To the formation of the general opinion of the future I dedicate this book.'[26]

Did success spoil Maynard Keynes? It was part of the Bloomsbury style, at once sly and outspoken, to suggest that of course it did. Jokes began to circulate about how grand 'Pozzo di Borgo' (Strachey's baroque usage) had become, with his posh friends and his reputedly huge income. True, Keynes became much better off, as he benefited from burgeoning literary earnings, which he managed himself with a keen eye and a firm hand. In 1918–19 his total income had been £1,800, two-thirds of it from his Treasury salary. A year later, his income was £5,156.

There are real difficulties in estimating how much such sums are worth at present-day values, either in pounds or in dollars. Admittedly, there are official indexes of consumer prices, which show that by the end of the century British prices were twenty times higher than in 1920 (a year of high but temporary inflation), thirty times higher than in 1930, and even a bit more compared with 1935. American prices, which fluctuated less, would by the early twenty-first century be about nine times higher than in 1920, ten times higher than in 1930, twelve times higher than in 1935.

So it seems simple to make calculations on this basis, and then convert sterling into dollars, which in 2009 means an exchange rate of around $1.50. This in itself is a striking change from $4.86 under the Gold Standard until 1931; but the two changes, of course, compensate for each other. Thus Keynes's income of £5,000 in 1920 could be expressed as the equivalent of some £150,000 or about $250,000 in today's money.

But this fails to capture the real value of what such an income was worth at the time. The official historian of the University of Cambridge gives the example of his own father, a successful college teaching Fellow who became a professor in due course, who in the early 1920s had an income a bit over £1,000 a year (and by the 1940s about £1,500). This was a basis on which to live well, supporting a wife and family in a select, convenient part of west Cambridge; with a comfortable house, purchased for £3,000 in the 1930s and worth far more than £1 million today, with its eight bedrooms, allowing for two maids; and boarding-school fees for three sons also found, albeit with some tight budgeting.[27]

In 1920, then, as a bachelor don, Keynes had an income several times higher than any Cambridge professor; and of this about three-quarters came from literary earnings. These continued at this high level for the next three years, boosted by the short book *A Revision of the Treaty* (1922). This was a sequel to *The Economic Consequences of the Peace* and Keynes compiled this sequel – some of it was adapted from earlier press articles – at the behest of his American publishers, Harcourt Brace. It was translated into French, German, Italian, Dutch, Swedish, Japanese and Russian. All this came before he was forty.

Different stories can be told about him. When the author of *The Economic Consequences of the Peace* fitted in a dutiful family visit to the home of his mother's brother in 1920, he was already a celebrity, certainly in the eyes of his fifteen-year-old cousin, who had never met him before. 'Maynard's name was on everyone's lips and in every paper one opened,' Neville Brown recalled. But he was emboldened none the less to show his cousin his school magazine, containing an article that he had himself written on the Versailles Treaty. The boy was charmed for life when, after studiously reading it, Maynard responded: 'Well, Neville, you know your policy is the same as mine.'[28] If Maynard performed more assertively in front of a man like Lytton Strachey, perhaps Pozzo was simply picking on someone of his own size.

For Keynes was not the only Bloomsbury author to have achieved widespread recognition. The tone of E. M. Forster's fiction, with the delicate touch of a moralist, had already acquired a devoted public before the war, especially in *A Room with a View* (1908) and *Howards End* (1910). His masterpiece, as many see it, *A Passage to India* (1924) was to follow before his career as a novelist in effect concluded.

Virginia Woolf had to wait longer. It was not until *Mrs Dalloway* (1925) that she achieved simultaneous publication in the United States, where she was ultimately to find such a warm reception as a feminist prophet. In *A Room of One's Own* (1929) she famously specified the conditions of emancipation as the room itself and £500 a year. But only from 1926 did her earnings, meticulously tabulated by Leonard, reach the magic figure. *To the Lighthouse* (1927) was her first big critical success, with 4,000 British sales and 8,000 American within six months. A year later, her playful, gender-challenging historical romp *Orlando* propelled her into a different league. 'This last half year I made over £1800,' she wrote in 1929; 'almost at the rate of £4000 a year; the salary almost of a Cabinet minister & time was, two years ago, when I toiled to make £200.'[29] She exaggerated the actual sums but captured the essence of the transformation. Her subsequent earnings of £1,000 or £2,000 a year were comparable with what Keynes was earning from his literary work in the late 1920s.

The defining event that had put Bloomsbury on the literary map was the publication of Lytton Strachey's *Eminent Victorians* in the spring of 1918. In distilling his critique of Victorian values through four exquisitely malicious biographical essays, Strachey conquered critical opinion with an unexpected ease that rather unnerved him. The turning point came specifically when Asquith, trailing the authority of an ex-prime minister, gave the prestigious Romanes Lecture at his old university, Oxford, in June 1918. He spoke of 'the most trenchant and brilliant series of biographical studies which I have read in a long time', paying tribute to 'Mr Strachey's subtle and suggestive art'.[30] That November an American edition of *Eminent Victorians* was published, followed by translations into Swedish, German, French, Italian and Spanish. For the rest of his life (he died in 1932) Strachey enjoyed an income of £2,000 to £3,000 a year – in a range somewhat higher than the literary earnings currently netted by either Woolf or Keynes.

The influence of the success of *Eminent Victorians* on the way that *The Economic Consequences of the Peace* was written, only a year later, seemed obvious to the friends of these close-knit Bloomsbury authors, vying for attention with each other. Keynes provided vivid, feline portraits of the Big Four that Strachey could not have bettered. Who can forget the aphorisms that, unfairly or not, characterise the leading players? 'One could not despise Clemenceau or dislike him, but only take a different view as to the nature of civilised man, or indulge, at least, a different hope,' was a deft introduction that paved the way to the verdict: 'He had one illusion – France; and one disillusion – mankind, including Frenchmen, and his colleagues not least.'[31]

The prior reputation of Woodrow Wilson was acknowledged by Keynes: 'Never had a philosopher held such weapons wherewith to bind the princes of this world.' It was acknowledged only to be deflated: 'The President was like a nonconformist minister, perhaps a Presbyterian.'[32] Here was a passage that Florence

Keynes, a connoisseur of Nonconformist susceptibilities, had tried to excise. Though the full portrait of Lloyd George had to wait until 1933 to be restored (and duly give the predictable offence), a few touches are left in the published book, where he is shown 'watching the company, with six or seven senses not available to ordinary men', prompting the worry 'that the poor President would be playing blind man's buff in that party'.[33]

The models to which Keynes turned for inspiration in *The Economic Consequences of the Peace* are not difficult to find. The way that the book begins, with an overview of the age that came to an end in 1914, is partly elegy and partly exposure of the complacent assumptions of the Victorian period. None of this was news to Bloomsbury. The way in which the naive idealism of Wilson was dissipated and foiled by the manoeuvres of Lloyd George and the bottomless cynicism of Clemenceau would have come as no surprise to readers of Henry James. 'The Old World was tough in wickedness anyhow,' Keynes confides, knowingly; 'the Old World's heart of stone might blunt the blade of the bravest knight-errant.'[34] Keynes makes a later comment that 'to suggest to the President that the treaty was an abandonment of his professions was to touch on the raw Freudian complex'.[35] This is certainly a Stracheyan insight, whether attributed to Lytton or to his younger brother James, already interested in Freud, whose English translator he became.

Keynes cultivated his Stracheyan side, publishing a collected volume, *Essays in Biography* (1933), with considerable success. This followed up on the acclaim for his *Essays in Persuasion* (1931), a collection of more polemical pieces from the previous decade or so. Though originally provoked by particular circumstances, the essays have more than ephemeral interest and remain, in many ways, the most accessible exposition of Keynes's views. These two volumes reached out to a public who, it is safe to suppose, would never even see, still less open, the two volumes of the *Treatise on*

Money (1930), Keynes's first solid book on economic theory. It was surely not the *Treatise* but the two volumes of essays that were responsible for boosting his literary earnings for the years 1932–4 to over £3,000 (at least £100,000 or $150,000 today). This was his best for ten years, and a nice offset to the effect of the slump on his income from the stock market.

Many of Keynes's essays had their origin as pamphlets or pieces written for periodicals. Some are short and serviceable; others contain aperçus and phrases that imperishably define their subjects. The most substantial of the biographical essays, in every sense, is the memoir of Alfred Marshall: homage, of course, to his old master on his death in 1924, and exquisitely wrought. Keynes was himself to depart from some of the Marshallian tenets in the next few years, but not in his endorsement of the view that 'the bare bones of economic theory are not worth much in themselves', except in so far as they yield practical conclusions: 'The whole point lies in applying them to the interpretation of current economic life.'[36]

Elsewhere, Keynes's own viewpoint on politics as on economics is readily disclosed. 'His temperament was naturally conservative,' he wrote in an essay on the recently deceased Asquith. 'With a little stupidity and a few prejudices dashed in he would have been Conservative in the political sense also. As it was, he was the perfect Whig for carrying into execution those Radical projects of his generation which were well judged.'[37]

What made Keynes's literary career distinctive was that he did not depend upon it as his sole, or even main, source of income. He became an active investor, managing his portfolio personally. From 1923 onward, this was how the bulk of his income was generated (except in 1932–3, when *Essays in Persuasion* kicked in). His total income was at a level around £4,000 to £7,000 a year for most of the 1920s and the early 1930s, with a dizzying peak of nearly £19,000 in 1937–8 – say three-quarters of a million pounds or certainly over a million dollars today. What underlay his income was the fluctuating performance of his investments.

Keynes was a risk-taker, with a penchant for currency speculation. In early 1920, with his profits as an author, he launched a syndicate with a scheme that he was sure would make his family and friends rich (as well as himself of course). He borrowed from his father and other members of his family to boost his own share of the risk, and roped in not only his brother Geoffrey but also Duncan Grant, who likewise financed his holdings with loans, from Vanessa Bell and other Bloomsbury friends. After fleeting initial success, the syndicate was wiped out within months, when the currencies misbehaved.

Maybe this simply went with the territory. But what is surely amazing is that his friends then let Keynes attempt to recoup – through essentially the same strategy, putting more of their money into currency speculation. And this he did, and with such success that by the end of 1922 he had cleared all his debts, both legal and moral, and had built up his personal holdings to over £20,000.

Keynes's net assets then tripled in value over the next two years, only to plummet to under £8,000 in 1929. The portfolio was then rebuilt, breasting half a million pounds at its peak in 1936 (say £20 million or $30 million today). Whereupon his net wealth fell (again), only to rise (again) during the Second World War.[38]

Keynes adopted a similar investment strategy as bursar, in managing the endowment of King's College. Here he was shackled by the college statutes, imposing institutional restraints against which he railed. He came up with the device in 1920 of establishing 'the Chest', in effect a capital fund that was free to be invested in the stock market. This was a regime – though sometimes questioned as to its strict legality under the statutes – under which the college's endowment flourished, so that by 1945 the Chest was worth about twelve times its original value. The effect was to switch the portfolio so far as possible out of land and trustee funds and into more profitable, if more risky, investments. A good strategy? The acid test was that other colleges in Cambridge followed suit.

The Cambridge oral tradition preserves many anecdotes about Keynes. One story has the following exchange. 'Mr Keynes, if businessmen are quite so stupid as you appear to believe, how do you suppose that they make money?' 'By competing against each other, of course!' He thought it worth an hour a day of his time, poring over the financial pages and telephoning his stockbroker, pitting his wits against the market. He also served from 1921 to 1938 as chairman of the National Mutual Assurance Company.

Keynes saw nothing wrong in making money. Nor did he see anything wrong in speculating or selling short, which he viewed as mechanisms for calibrating a market that would, as he well knew, punish those who read it wrongly. He had his share of disasters, amid which he remained remarkably detached and resilient. There were more ups than downs and he became wealthy in the process: if not seriously rich by the standards of the City of London then certainly by the standards of Bloomsbury or Cambridge.

Little wonder that he did not live like the average professor of economics. Indeed he never became a professor in the British sense, and his riposte, when described as 'Professor Keynes', was to say that he would not accept the indignity without the emoluments. He could literally afford to say this because he did not need the emoluments after 1920. So he was able to buy his freedom of action by retaining his Fellowship at King's on much his own terms. He escaped a lot of routine teaching but still offered lectures annually in the Economics Faculty. He also continued as editor of the *Economic Journal*, the leading British periodical in the field. He had been put into this post in 1912 – the board was chaired by Marshall – at the age of twenty-eight, at first with some oversight on account of his youth, but from 1919 to 1945 in undisputed command. This gave him great influence within the economics profession.

And his own writings, both journalism and solid books, continued to be published all the while. The editorship, like the bursarship, was an onerous post which many others in his shoes would have made into virtually a full-time job, or one held only for a few years, or at any rate one that its holder surrendered once the call into government service came. Not Keynes: a busy man who found time to pursue several careers simultaneously.

2

'On the extreme left of celestial space'
John Maynard Keynes, 1924–1946

M AYNARD HAD BEEN brought up in a household with every academic door invitingly ajar, just waiting to be pushed, but with few windows open on the arts. His brother Geoffrey, who became an expert on the drawings of William Blake and was to serve as chairman of the National Portrait Gallery, recalled that, when the boys were young, their 'home surroundings afforded no aesthetic stimulus of modernity or novelty'.[1] Yet as young men they both reached out beyond the cultural presuppositions of Harvey Road. For example, they shared a passion for the ballet. The bravura style of Serge Diaghilev's productions, as seen in London from 1911, captivated both. Geoffrey eventually responded by composing a ballet himself, *Job*, produced in 1931 and based on Blake's illustrations. Maynard's response was dramatic in another sense; in 1925 he married a ballerina.

Falling for an attractive dancer, of course, can mean many things. Maynard's relationship with Lydia Lopokova meant a further extension of his cultural hinterland – beyond the extension that Bloomsbury had already given him. Lest he be stereotyped as simply an academic figure, it should be remembered how he developed close friendships with non-academic writers, as we have seen. Lest he be seen as purely literary in his cultural tastes, it should be remembered that he became friends with active artists and also with art critics like Clive Bell and Roger Fry. It was the exhibition that Fry mounted in 1910, 'Manet and the Post-Impressionists', that effectively introduced the London public to Post-Impressionism and its Bloomsbury patrons alike. Keynes supported all of this financially and, during the First World War, began serious collecting himself on visits to Paris. Though small, his collection included works by Braque, Cézanne, Matisse and Picasso; he later lent them freely for exhibition during the Second World War; and many of them are now on public display in Cambridge at the Fitzwilliam Museum.

For obvious reasons, Maynard was a patron of the paintings of his Bloomsbury friends. He had a close and passionate relationship with Duncan Grant, one of whose best works is his portrait of the young Keynes. Vanessa Bell, a painter herself, became a friend of Maynard's through Bloomsbury; and it was when Vanessa succeeded in seducing Duncan that Maynard had to accept that their own homosexual relationship was over. But they all remained friends, albeit on Bloomsbury terms that allowed a good deal of latitude for bitchy gossip, some of it, behind Maynard's back, about Lydia. By January 1922 Duncan was writing to Vanessa: 'As for Maynard, until I see him carrying on with L. I must give up trying to imagine what happens – it beggars my fancy.'[2]

Lydia Lopokova had made her first London appearances with Diaghilev's company in 1918, weeks before the end of the war. We know that Maynard met her then; that he went backstage; that he told Duncan Grant that he was offered the opportunity to pinch the legs of the vivacious and uninhibited Russian ballerina; and that he remarked that this offer would have appealed more to the unambiguously heterosexual Clive Bell.[3] This was hardly the stuff of romance, especially since Lydia had for two years been married to Diaghilev's business manager, a much older man.

How different, then, by January 1922! By now she had abruptly walked out on both Diaghilev and her husband (a bigamist, as it turned out) before returning to the former but not the latter.

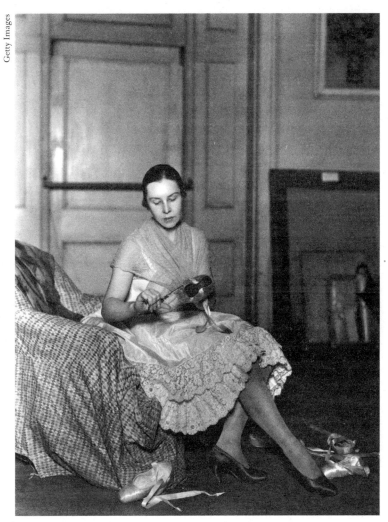

Lydia Lopokova at the end of her career as a ballerina,
as Maynard must have seen her in the 1920s.

At twenty-nine, she was at the peak of her career. She was now treated as a celebrity – but so, in his way, was the thirty-eight-year-old economist who became her greatest fan.

Alas, Diaghilev's revival of Tchaikovsky's *Sleeping Beauty* failed to pull in a postwar crowd for whom its unabashed romanticism was altogether too much. But Keynes sat there, night by night, in the half-empty stalls, with eyes only for Lopokova. 'One of her new charms,' he reported to Vanessa, 'is the most knowing and judicious use of English words.'4 Vanessa told him firmly to have her as a mistress, not a wife. But the charms of Lydiaspeak quickly proved irresistible. 'I gobble you my dear Maynard,' wrote Lydia. 'I am not like you talented in idea put into words, I express myself better in impulses to you.'5

Lydia's impulses were to be life-sustaining for Maynard, literally so in the later years when he was a sick man. Their marriage in 1925 gave him a new focus, a new emotional stability and a sheer delight of which he never wearied. Like Duncan Grant, like Lytton Strachey – two homosexual partners in his formative years – Maynard Keynes thus entered a successful long-term heterosexual relationship. Its manifest success owed much to Lydia's uninhibited sensuality, not least in removing Maynard's feelings of sexual insecurity. Their failure to have children was not for want of trying.

Lydia was not easily accepted by Bloomsbury. The more gracious of Maynard's old friends, like Morgan (E. M.) Forster, lived to lament how badly they had underestimated her. But the Bells never really relented, with long-term effects in perpetuating their own family view of the Keyneses. The result was not only to leave a scornful and misleading impression of bird-brained Lydia but also to exaggerate in retrospect the depth and permanence of Maynard's alleged alienation from Bloomsbury during the last twenty years of his life.

True, there were some big and obvious changes. When Lydia moved into 46 Gordon Square, she hated the gaudy frescoes that Vanessa Bell and Duncan Grant had painted. These were whitewashed over – naturally enough, one might think, as Lydia sought to make it her own home. But in old Bloomsbury such actions were viewed as hardly less than cultural war-crimes, and Maynard was no longer the Bells' automatically welcome guest.

In a former era, he had written much of *The Economic Consequences of the Peace* sitting in the garden of their farmhouse, Charleston, near Lewes in Sussex. This was the country home established by the Bells with Duncan Grant as a live-in member of the ménage. It was at the foot of the lane leading to Charleston, on one occasion at the end of the First World War, that a painting by Cézanne was left in the hedge when the official car of the Chancellor of the Exchequer had dropped off Keynes on his return from a Paris visit.

Charleston, and the nearby village of Firle, was thus Bell territory. But, once married, Keynes acquired his own country home – Tilton House, an old farmhouse with garden in the same parish of Firle as Charleston, and thus only a mile or so away along the lane. The Bells huffily talked of moving away, perhaps to East Anglia, but eventually stayed put in their own house, just as in London they now had their own residence at 37 Gordon Square. Virginia and Leonard Woolf were by this time established at 52 Tavistock Square, around the corner in Bloomsbury; and their country home at Rodmell in Sussex was only a few miles from Firle. Thus, like it or not, many of the core members of Bloomsbury continued to live in close proximity, whether in town or in the country. Why did they do it if their friendship had in fact ended? Was the property market in England really so constricted in the options available?

Common sense as well as clear documentation points to the obvious answer. Yes, the Bells refused to grant proper diplomatic recognition of the Keyneses' marriage. But, more important surely, the two figures of real genius in Bloomsbury – Virginia Woolf and Maynard Keynes – maintained and sustained a warm relationship underpinned by a mutual respect that each continued to need and value. On being shown part of Keynes's *A Tract on Monetary Reform* in 1923, Woolf simply wrote that 'the process of mind there displayed is as far ahead of me as Shakespeare's'. Such a tribute surely registers in our minds even when we read her characteristic addendum: 'True, I don't respect it so much.'[6]

The influence of Leonard Woolf, at once Maynard's old friend and his current collaborator in public life, obviously helped matters. But the presence of Lydia does not appear to have detracted from the meetings of 'two couples, elderly, childless, distinguished' (as Virginia put it in 1928, when the eldest of them was still under fifty). She commented on Maynard's table talk that it was 'always the proof of a remarkable mind when it overflows thus vigorously into bypaths'. And on Lydia she simply recorded something that has too often been omitted from the Bloomsbury biographies: 'She says very sensible things.'[7] The Woolfs and the Keyneses used to meet regularly around Christmas – obviously a special time in England for seeing intimate friends. In fact, in every year but one during the last decade of Virginia's life, there was a reunion of the four of them – the last on Christmas Eve 1940. Within a year, Virginia had drowned herself in the River Ouse near Rodmell.

Such were the friendships that mattered most to the author of the *General Theory*. As Lydia said of one politician who dared criticise her adored husband, 'he does not know that it is poor of him not to allow you to be more than economist, all your "walks of life" make a piquant personality'.[8] She knew better. And her influence led him further in such walks.

Naturally Maynard supported Lydia's own career, which, after she ceased dancing, was as an actress. She performed professionally until Maynard's heart condition worsened in the late 1930s. Lydia often stayed in Bloomsbury whenever Maynard was in Cambridge during the academic term, the two of them exchanging letters every day. They worked together in helping to establish the Camargo

Society as a ballet company in 1930; and on its demise in 1933 its assets passed to the Vic-Wells Ballet and thence to the Royal Ballet. This was an important lifeline at a time when the very survival of professional ballet in Britain was at risk, and it was not Keynes's only initiative in support of the performing arts.

'I gave rather a good lecture this morning,' Maynard wrote to Lydia from Cambridge one day in November 1933. 'Since then I've been amusing myself thinking out a plan to build a small, very smart, modern theatre for the College. Will you agree to appear in the first performance if it comes off?'[9] This was the origin of the Arts Theatre, which opened in Cambridge on 3 February 1936, the night before the *General Theory* was published. The theatre was largely financed by Keynes himself in the end because it proved difficult to dispose of preference shares during the Depression. He cheerfully took up the slack, thinking it one of the comforts of being a rich man that he could afford to do so.

His view of what mattered in the long run was shown in his essay 'Economic possibilities for our grandchildren', later published in *Essays in Persuasion*. It was first drafted as a talk in 1928, at a time when it is probable that Lydia's recent miscarriage already meant that they would have no children of their own. Personally disappointed in his hopes of progeny, Keynes none the less kept the same title for the essay when it was first published in late 1930. Even when confronted with a world sliding into depression, he looked beyond the immediate economic difficulties that confronted 'man' (using the gendered terminology of that era). The real problem, then, was 'how to use his freedom from pressing economic cares, how to occupy the leisure, which science and compound interest will have won for him, to live wisely and agreeably and well'. And under those conditions, love of money in itself 'will be recognised for what it is, a somewhat disgusting morbidity, one of those semi-criminal, semi-pathological propensities which one hands over with a shudder to the specialists in mental disease'.[10]

Keynes was not turning his back on either economics or economic criteria in saying such things. 'Poverty is a great evil,' he wrote in 1933; 'and economic advantage is a real good, not to be sacrificed to alternative real goods unless it is clearly of an inferior weight.'[11] But he followed this by challenging conventional conceptions of what would 'pay' – and doing so, of course, right at the bottom of the world slump. 'We are capable of shutting off the sun and the stars because they do not pay a dividend,' he expostulated. 'London is one of the richest cities in the history of civilization, but it cannot "afford" the highest standards of achievement of which its own living citizens are capable, because they do not "pay".'[12] Nor was this a sort of siege mentality, even though Keynes was currently in a rather protectionist mood. 'Ideas, knowledge, art, hospitality, travel – these are the things which should of their nature be international.'[13]

It was congruent with his own sense of values that he was to play a crucial role in the foundation of the Arts Council as a publicly funded umbrella organisation supporting the arts in Britain. That he did so during the most stressful years of the Second World War is doubly remarkable: first because he thought this an appropriate time for such a commitment to be made, and secondly because he himself stole some of his precious time from other government business to make it happen. This was how the Covent Garden Opera House received its first subvention from public funds at the end of the war. Keynes was by then chairman of both the new Arts Council and the Covent Garden trustees, thus responsible for both sides of the transaction. In February 1946 he and Lydia received the king and queen at Covent Garden for a gala performance by the Sadler's Wells Ballet, as what Keynes called 'a landmark in the restoration of English cultural life'.[14] The production was of *The Sleeping Beauty*, in which Maynard had watched Lydia dance some twenty-four years previously.

*   *   *

'Words ought to be a little wild,' Keynes once claimed, 'for they are the assaults of thoughts upon the unthinking.'[15] It was journalism that knitted together so many of Keynes's talents. His capacity for effective writing, reaching out to assault a public that never read the *Economic Journal*, thus helped him to communicate his ideas. Nor was this simply a matter of popularising concepts that he had already evolved in his academic work. Instead, the effort of projecting his meaning to a lay public would sometimes prompt an aphorism that was more than just a happy choice of words: it might hold an insight that then fed back into his thinking about fundamental economic theory. In this endeavour he was no doubt encouraged by the high fees that he could command; but his real drive was surely political, in seeking to change the agenda of politics through reasoned debate that would create a new climate of public opinion.

It was natural that the author of *The Economic Consequences of the Peace* should be asked to contribute newspaper articles in the ensuing debate about the Versailles Peace Treaty and reparations. This was the origin of Keynes's connection with the *Manchester Guardian*, by then already established as the greatest Liberal newspaper in Britain under the legendary fifty-year editorship of C. P. Scott. The big commission was for a series of supplements on the economic condition of postwar Europe, which appeared in 1922, with an editorial fee of £200 per issue (say £7,000 or $10,000 today). Scott's dictum, that comment is free but facts are sacred, suited Keynes well since he had plenty of both to offer his readers. He also became the *Manchester Guardian*'s special correspondent at the international conference at Genoa, summoned by Lloyd George to discuss European economic reconstruction in April 1922. Keynes's articles were syndicated abroad, notably through the *World* in New York to newspapers across the United States.

Back in Bloomsbury, where Lydia had already taken up residence, she immediately started reading the *Manchester*

Guardian every day. She told Maynard what a thrill it was to see 'you in M.G. quite a big photo. Very famous!' She assured him that 'it is very nice to meet your articles they *breathe* to me'. And when he evidently uttered some sort of depreciation of his efforts, drawing on his reserves of false modesty, she reprimanded him. 'Do not speak against your articles in journalism – just think how many peoples read, understand and remember it; and when you go to bed have the feeling of the work you have done with mind and inspiration.'[16] This was not only just what Keynes wanted to hear; it was just what he needed to hear. His academic friends in Cambridge or his fastidious intellectual friends in Bloomsbury might disparage his journalism as a waste of his time, but Lydia saw the obvious.

The sheer hard work in fulfilling this commission was a good investment. It was the origin of Keynes's book *A Tract on Monetary Reform* (1923). At this time Keynes was still a convinced free-trader and wrote as such in the Liberal weekly paper the *Nation* during the general election of 1923. He convinced at least one reader. 'Protection as a cure for unemployment! *ç'a n'existe pas*!' wrote Lydia. 'When you speak about our imports as our incomes etc. it seems to me a suicide not to trade free. Life without incomes is deplorable.'[17] It would be pretentious to rephrase this as the germ of an idea that if we cut back consumption we cut back effective demand; but Lydia's ingenuous comment lacks erudition rather than understanding. It graphically shows us – and it showed Maynard – how his ideas were received by an untutored but not unintelligent reading public.

The *Tract* became a plea for monetary stability. This was not surprising given the effects of acute monetary instability in postwar Europe. The notorious German inflation, with its wheelbarrows full of marks, was the most vividly memorable example. But Britain too had experienced a burst of inflation, which had been brought down by the authorities, using their traditional weapon of high interest rates or 'dear money'. Though Keynes is usually thought of as an advocate of cheap money, he had supported dear money at the moment when it seemed to be a necessary corrective. It was, again, his *The Economic Consequences of the Peace* that had put into general circulation a subsequently famous quotation: 'Lenin is said to have declared that the best way to destroy the capitalist system was to debauch the currency.'[18]

So Keynes needed no convincing that stability was in itself a good thing. But in the *Tract* he was already contesting the conventional view that stability could be achieved only by restoring the Gold Standard, meaning that the currency would have a set value in gold, thus fixing its parity against other currencies on the Gold Standard. How would this fixed parity translate into domestic prices? Only by allowing the free inflow and outflow of gold reserves to produce consequent effects on all other prices, by either inflating or deflating them. So ran the orthodox answer.

But Keynes had another answer. He was now ready to explore the alternative of working from the other end of the problem: stabilising prices at home by managing the parity of the currency on the international exchanges. This could be done, he thought, by the active intervention of each country's central bank. In arguing this out in the *Tract*, Keynes moved into the centre of a public debate on economic policy and helped shift its focus from Free Trade to monetary policy.

The *Tract* both is and is not an easy read. Not, for obvious reasons: just look at the pages of tables with dense columns showing such things as purchasing power parity or exchange quotations in London one month forward. This is not everyone's cup of tea. Yet, compared with most treatments of such issues, the book is composed with a lambent lucidity. It starts on its first page with a simple proposition – 'Money is only important for what it will procure' – that leads into an accessible exposition of not only the technical problems but the underlying theory. Again we can look at the reaction of one loyal reader in Bloomsbury. 'I told them that I reached the "Quantity Theory of Money" moment and could not continue and yet could not follow your suggestion that all unintellectual readers may close their eyes for this especial chapter,' wrote Lydia. 'I did not tell them, but I feel that if I escape this chapter I am not an advanced person. How painful would to become such!'[19]

Keynes's career in journalism included, in effect, the acquisition of his own weekly paper. The *Nation* had been strongly identified with the New Liberalism before the war but faced an uncertain future after it. As a result of Keynes's involvement from 1922 with the Liberal summer school, an annual gathering in Oxford or Cambridge to debate Liberal policy, he became part of a consortium that took over the financially failing *Nation*. He was himself a major investor, became chairman of the reconstituted board, put in his Cambridge colleague Hubert Henderson as editor – in short, took charge and wielded the new broom.

Keynes kept on only one of the team of regular contributors: Leonard Woolf, who took on the post of literary editor after an attempt to employ T. S. Eliot faltered. The *Nation* naturally became, in its back section, virtually a Bloomsbury house organ, with contributions from Clive Bell, Morgan Forster, Lytton Strachey and, of course, the literary editor's wife. In 1931 it was to merge with the *New Statesman*, a product of the Fabian Society and generally in support of the Labour Party. Keynes continued to be a frequent contributor until 1939 and served as chairman of the combined board until his death.

Why did he do all this? True, he liked to have a finger in every pie, he enjoyed dispensing patronage, he looked after his Bloomsbury friends in the process and he had ample means to finance his little hobby. But the overriding reason is surely that his activities in journalism served his own political agenda. The *Nation* and subsequently the *New Statesman* guaranteed him a platform for his more serious reflections on economics and politics.

Keynes also reached out to a more popular readership. Though his journalistic career was first launched through the highbrow *Manchester Guardian*, his own press articles were latterly more likely to appear in London in the *Evening Standard*, owned by the maverick Canadian press baron Lord Beaverbrook. Beaverbrook was an imperialist and a supporter of what he called Empire Free Trade – a new name at this juncture for the protectionist policies that the Conservatives had been peddling for the past twenty years. None of this was to Keynes's taste; but Beaverbrook was tolerant of dissent from the bright young men who wrote in his papers; and, because he despised Free Trade, he was suspicious of its twin orthodoxy, the Gold Standard. So when, in July 1925, *The Times* turned down three articles by Keynes attacking the return to the Gold Standard, Beaverbrook snapped them up for the *Evening Standard*.

This was the origin of Keynes's pamphlet 'The Economic Consequences of Mr Churchill' (1925). It was republished in the United States as 'The Economic Consequences of Sterling Parity' – presumably because educated Americans might have heard of the clever Mr Keynes but were unclear about this Mr Churchill. Keynes's pamphlet 'The Means to Prosperity' (1933) had a rather similar origin. It was likewise offered as a series of articles to *The Times* in London, which accepted on this occasion, and the subsequent pamphlet was republished in the United States.

Keynes manifested a fairly consistent political outlook, from the period before the First World War to the end of the Second World War. 'Am I a Liberal?' was the title of an article he published in the *Nation* in 1925. It was a good question in an era when the historic Liberal Party was busily destroying itself and the Labour Party had not yet emerged as a broad-based alternative to the Conservatives, who therefore dominated British politics for a generation. 'If one is a political animal, it is most uncomfortable not to belong to a political party,' Keynes began, stating what he regarded as obvious. The Conservatives made absolutely no appeal to him – 'I should not be amused or excited or edified.' If it was a sort of emotional snobbery that kept him from being a Conservative, it was a sort of intellectual snobbery that kept him from identifying with Labour. Confessing that 'I do not believe that the intellectual elements in the Labour Party will ever exercise adequate control', he turned to the Liberal Party as 'still the best instrument of future progress – if only it had strong leadership and the right programme'.[20]

So Keynes applied himself in the late 1920s to remedying these two deficiencies. He saw the remedy for each very clearly; and in each case it involved a painful new departure for traditional Liberals. The leadership had to come from the most dynamic figure in British politics: Lloyd George, of course. In a party that had been riven for nearly a decade by a conflict between Asquith and Lloyd George, it was difficult to heal the wounds, difficult to forget or forgive. Keynes was a natural Asquithian and a prominent critic of Lloyd George's conduct over the peace treaty. Nonetheless he came to see Lloyd George as the man to back, and he did so because the two of them saw eye to eye on the need to make unemployment the programme on which the Liberals should now be fighting.

When Keynes published his article 'Does unemployment need a drastic remedy?' in the *Nation* in May 1924, it attracted considerable attention. Keynes cited an official figure of 770,000 unemployed adult males – lower than in the previous couple of years but historically high. These official figures counted only the workers under the National Insurance system, first introduced in 1911 but subsequently expanded in coverage. By this measure unemployment stood at over 10 per cent in 1924; a modern estimate would suggest about 7 per cent of the total workforce.[21] But 10 per cent was the figure that shocked contemporaries. It was double what had been accepted as normal before the First World War.

It was in this context that Keynes picked up a hint from Lloyd George in advocating 'national development' as a remedy. For the first time we can recognise the distinctive voice that we now call Keynesian, in his plea that 'we must look for succour to the principle that *prosperity is cumulative*. We have stuck in a rut. We need an impulse, a jolt, an acceleration.' It was not so much a policy as a mindset. 'There may be stimulating medicines which are wholesome,' he asserted, simply as a precept. 'Business is weighed down by timidity,' he reported, deploring the baleful mood that held back investment. 'No one is ready to plant seeds which only a long summer can bring to fruit.' The article is infused with a restless conviction that this is none the less the moment of opportunity.[22]

Here was the beginning of the new agenda, and of the personal reconciliation that was to make it practical politics. When Lloyd George met Keynes at an official dinner the same week, the Welsh charmer took the opportunity for a little flattery, saying loudly to another guest: 'I approve Keynes, because, whether he is right or wrong, he is always dealing with realities.'[23] After this, the way was smooth for further co-operation. For Keynes it entailed a wrenching break with Asquith, still nominally the leader of a nominally reunited Liberal Party. It was Asquith's hard line against the General Strike of 1926 that brought the final breach. Keynes used the *Nation* to make clear that, whatever the past misdemeanours that factional Asquithians insisted on dragging up from the Versailles era, he thought that Lloyd George's more conciliatory position towards trade union members was now correct.

For Keynes it was axiomatically desirable that Liberals and Labour should work together. After all, they had done so, to very constructive effect, in the progressive alliance that had governed

British politics in the pre-war period. Why not again in the late 1920s? He argued that Liberals were 'inclined to sympathise with Labour about what is just' but to disagree on the effective means of achieving it without sacrificing efficiency. Labour's problem was that its adherents were so old-fashioned. 'They respond to anti-communist rubbish with anti-capitalist rubbish,' he claimed. 'I do not believe that class war or nationalisation is attractive or stimulating to modern minds.'[24] His own view was that 'capitalism, wisely managed, can probably be made more efficient for attaining economic ends than any alternative system yet in sight, but that in itself it is in many ways extremely objectionable'.[25] Cloaking essentially the same proposition in a different rhetoric, Keynes put forward his constructive alternative: 'The true socialism of the future will emerge, I think, from an endless variety of experiments directed towards discovering the respective appropriate sphere of the individual and the social, and the terms of a fruitful alliance between these sister instincts.'[26]

Keynes's economic agenda came as an attack on the free-market doctrines of the day, yet it did not come from a socialist. He wanted to reconcile socialists to the existing system by ameliorating its unfairness and, in this sense, to save capitalism from itself. For Keynes had a lifelong belief in the unique virtues of the market – if only it could be made to work properly. He regarded comprehensive nationalisation as a lamentable irrelevance. Indeed he thought that many of the socialist mantras of his day remained fixated on the problems of Marx's era, the era that had closed in the year of his own birth.

'The republic of my imagination lies on the extreme left of celestial space,' Keynes said, teasingly.[27] His radicalism, then, was of the intellect not of the barricades or the class war. He saw antiquated anti-capitalist dogma as no better than the dogma of laissez-faire, which emerged as his prime target.

*   *   *

In politics, he tried and failed. Lloyd George largely accepted an agenda that we can justifiably call Keynesian in his attempt to spearhead a Liberal revival. His manifesto for the 1929 general election was boldly titled *We Can Conquer Unemployment*. Keynes responded, in collaboration with Hubert Henderson of the *Nation*, by issuing a widely cited pamphlet, 'Can Lloyd George Do It?'. The correct answer was yes, of course. But the election itself, fought under the first-past-the-post system, showed that winning 24 per cent of the vote gave the Liberal Party only 59 seats in the House of Commons; whereas Labour with 37 per cent of the popular vote ended up with 287 MPs. Keynes had said that he preferred the Liberals because they were not a class-based party; but this meant that their vote was spread too evenly to maximise their representation. The fact was that, for the next half-century, the class-based allegiances of Labour and the Conservatives were to dominate electoral politics in Britain.

True, the Conservatives had lost office. But the experience of two years of minority Labour government now showed that the Liberals, though supposedly holding the balance of power, had insufficient clout to realise Keynes's hopes of providing a progressive alternative. The financial crisis of August 1931 spiralled into a political crisis that brought down the government, only for the Labour Prime Minister, Ramsay MacDonald, to soldier on as head of a so-called National Government (mainly and increasingly Conservative). Formed to defend the Gold Standard, one of its first acts was to abandon it; the pound sterling collapsed in September 1931. A general election in the next month gave an overwhelming majority for the National Government, which was to remain in office until the Second World War. These were traumatising, polarising events.

Amid these changes, Keynes showed himself willing to change his mind about tariffs. For politicians, inconsistency is one of the worst charges to face, and generally has to be dissimulated. Thus when Keynes entered the political arena he was held to the same standard. After all, he had been an orthodox free-trader as late as the mid-1920s; yet by 1930 his policy advice to government allowed for the relevance of tariffs in Britain's economic predicament. Crucially, in March 1931 he made this public in a widely noticed article in the *New Statesman*, 'Proposals for a revenue tariff', which he republished in *Essays in Persuasion* at the end of that year, and whether this was a tariff for revenue or protection seemed a fine distinction to many. Moreover, he made it all worse by further *New Statesman* articles in 1933 under the rubric 'National self-sufficiency'. The evidence on inconsistency is overwhelming: guilty as charged.

The Cambridge oral tradition provides a pithy riposte to all this. Yes, Keynes is often quoted as saying, 'When the facts change, I change my mind – what do you do, sir?' The facts had indeed changed, to an appreciable extent. Free Trade had

David Low, Solo Syndication / Associated Newspapers Ltd.

In an unpublished cartoon from 1929, Low shows Keynes and Lloyd George trying to get the lifeboat afloat, in opposition to the Treasury with Winston Churchill at the helm.

formerly paralleled the Gold Standard in sustaining self-acting, free-market principles in international trade. The British people were accustomed to congratulate themselves for adopting a system that was simultaneously enlightened, impartial, just – and to their material advantage. Free Trade had thus brought prosperity to those who preached it.

But all this had changed by 1931. The discipline of maintaining the Gold Standard through high interest rates brought the pain of persistent and rising unemployment. So it was not surprising that hard times fostered the cry for tariffs, to protect British jobs. If something had to give, it was better, surely, to part with the old Free Trade orthodoxy than the Gold Standard itself. Such were the feelings of many Liberals by early 1931; but of course the abandonment of the Gold Standard that September then rendered this argument largely obsolete. Yet Keynes was egregious in maintaining his new-found sympathy for tariffs at this juncture.

The reason has to be more than a tactical policy shift, dependent on strictly economic reasoning. We should remember that he could not have introduced his stimulus proposals of 1924 because of the return to the Gold Standard (which did not happen until a year later). Likewise, Keynes did not simply drop his tariff proposals with Britain's departure from the Gold Standard in 1931. This is a problem that we shall need to address further in Chapter 3, in assessing the practical constraints under which Keynes worked in offering policy advice on how to tackle unemployment.

What is already clear is that Keynes was neither a dogmatic adherent of Free Trade nor a reliable convert to the merits of protection. But the slump that was ravaging the world economy by 1933 certainly fed into his disillusion with international financial orthodoxies. 'The divorce between ownership and the real responsibility of management is serious within a country when, as a result of joint-stock enterprise, ownership is broken up between innumerable individuals who buy their interest today and sell it tomorrow and lack altogether both knowledge and responsibility towards what they momentarily own,' wrote Keynes. 'But when the same principle is applied internationally, it is, in times of stress, intolerable – I am irresponsible towards what I own and those who operate what I own are irresponsible towards me.'[28] Such a system now stood as a self-evident failure. 'It is not intelligent, it is not beautiful, it is not just, it is not virtuous – and it doesn't deliver the goods.'[29]

Keynes was not the only British citizen, certainly not the only Liberal, to feel cut adrift in hostile seas. With the world plunging into depression, the appeal of political extremists was highlighted by events in Germany, where Hitler's march to power became unstoppable. In Britain, as in the United States, many young people interpreted the crisis as heralding the death throes of capitalism and looked for salvation to communism instead – as Keynes was very well aware, very close to home. Vanessa Bell's son Julian, who had gone up to King's College, Cambridge, as an undergraduate in 1929, later explained that he and his contemporaries had had little interest in politics – 'we almost all of us had implicit confidence in Maynard Keynes's rosy prophecies of continually increasing capitalist prosperity.' By 1933, all that had changed, as the well-connected young man declared in an article which he found no difficulty in getting published in the *New Statesman*: 'It is not so much that we are all Socialists now as that we are all Marxists now.'[30]

Keynes had never had much time for Marx. The thrilling rhetoric of the young Marx, stressing human volition in remaking society, was little known until the early writings were rediscovered and widely disseminated in the 1960s. So the Marx whom Keynes rejected was a determinist economist who predicted that capitalism could not survive its own internal contradictions. Of *Das Kapital* Keynes flatly declared to the veteran socialist Bernard Shaw: 'I am sure that its contemporary *economic* value (apart from occasional but inconstructive and discontinuous flashes of insight) is *nil*.'[31] If the Soviet Union was the Marxist word made flesh, as communists argued, so much the worse for a regime in which free criticism had been stifled, only to produce incompetence. 'Let Stalin be a terrifying example to all who seek to make experiments,' wrote Keynes in 1933, even before the show trials replenished the gulag archipelago.[32]

The fact remained that it was capitalism that was now on trial. Moreover, like all political reformists, Keynes needed to show that reform of the system was indeed possible. Yet the experience of the Labour Government – inept and irresolute – hardly provided reassurance that it could cope with the problems it faced from the malfunctioning of a system in which socialists said they did not believe anyway. On the key issue of unemployment policy, Keynes had found only one Labour minister on his wavelength – the wrong minister, as it turned out, since Sir Oswald Mosley, though a vibrant and charismatic presence, soon tired of Labour's machinations. Mosley eventually opted for an alternative career path as Britain's Mussolini-in-waiting, complete with fetching black shirt.

Mosley's British Union of Fascists was manifestly in favour of stimulating everything in sight, from anti-Semitism to the British economy. Equally manifest was its lack of political appeal for Keynes and his Bloomsbury friends, who spent much of the 1930s fighting fascism with their typewriters – or, more nobly, in the case of Julian Bell, by putting his life at stake in the Spanish Civil War. When young Julian was killed in 1937, Keynes wrote a short memoir for the King's College magazine, reprinted in the collected edition of the *Essays in Biography*. This moving and generous appreciation of her nephew pleased Virginia Woolf – 'reluctant as I am to recognise your gift in that line,' she explained to the author, 'when it seems obvious that nature gave me none for mathematics.'[33]

Julian Bell was almost like family to Maynard, who respected without sharing the beliefs for which the young man had died. Personal sympathy thus informs Keynes's public remarks, often surprisingly indulgent to Marxists. For instance, in 1939 he qualified the general case he made, that a consensus to reform the system could be reached between small-l liberals in all parties, by adding: 'There is no one in politics today worth sixpence outside the ranks of the liberals except the post-war generation of intellectual Communists under thirty-five.'[34]

The essential problem, then, was to mobilise the latent liberalism to which Keynes appealed. He was confident that this could be done, but was disparaging about his own record in actually doing so. When he published *Essays in Persuasion* in 1931, the preface stated: 'Here are collected the croakings of twelve years – the croakings of a Cassandra who could never influence the course of events in time.'[35]

Having failed, his response was to try again. Keynes remained, in short, a progressive who naturally looked for allies on the left; and he remained a liberal even after he had despaired of the British Liberal Party. So the options remained essentially the same, in bad times as in good. All that had changed in Britain was that liberal opinion now had to be mobilised mainly through the Labour Party, with all its flaws but also with all its natural advantages in representing the under-privileged many rather than the privileged few. 'In this country henceforward power will normally reside with the Left,' wrote Keynes in 1934. 'The Labour Party will always have a majority, except when something has happened to raise a doubt in the minds of reasonable and disinterested persons whether the Labour Party are in the right.'[36]

Keynes wrote this at a time when the Right had about 520 out of 600 MPs in the House of Commons and Labour had about 50. Clearly the man was an optimist about the future course of British politics. Clearly, too, he found the course of politics in the

United States of the New Deal a good deal more immediately encouraging. Not until 1945, at the end of the Second World War, did Labour come into the political inheritance that Keynes saw as part of the natural order of things after 1931. At the time of the general election of 1935, the leader of the Liberal Party, Sir Herbert Samuel, received a rebuff when he sought a campaign contribution for the party from the wealthy economist who had been one of its most prominent backers only a few years before. 'But, alas, I scarcely know where I stand,' Keynes wrote back, with no cheque in the envelope. 'Somewhere, I suppose, between Liberal and Labour, though in some respects to the left of the latter, not feeling that anyone just now really represents my strongest convictions.'[37]

The more fundamental point is how Keynes envisaged the process of conquering public opinion. His view here has often been caricatured, not least by himself. Again, what he told his friends, when he read 'My Early Beliefs' to the memoir club, has often been quoted against him: that 'we repudiated all versions of the doctrine of original sin, of there being insane and irrational springs of wickedness in most men'; and that 'we completely misunderstood human nature, including our own'. Keynes added, even in 1938: 'I still suffer incurably from attributing an unreal rationality to other people's feelings and behaviour (and doubtless to my own, too).'[38] Put this together with those famous 'presuppositions of Harvey Road' and you have a Keynes who remains a political innocent, with an alarmingly naive view of how democracy really works.

Yes and no. Since he said most of this himself, it suggests a degree of self-knowledge. He had, after all, been in the Treasury during the First World War and learned a good deal about the actual workings of government. His experience of the Paris peace conference led him to formalise his view that there existed two sorts of opinion: 'the outside and the inside; the opinion of the public voiced by the politicians and the newspapers, and the opinion of the politicians, the journalists and the civil servants, upstairs and backstairs and behind-stairs, expressed in limited circles'. And he said this, not privately in a cynical moment, but publicly in *The Revision of the Treaty* (1922).[39] It surely provides a key to understanding Keynes's answer, in 1934, to the question: Why had he failed so far? 'Because I have not yet succeeded in convincing either the expert or the ordinary man that I am right,' he explained, adding: 'It is, I feel certain, only a matter of time before I convince both; and when both are convinced, economic policy will, with the usual time lag, follow suit.'[40]

So Keynes refused to accept the Marxist analysis that of course he would go on failing in a capitalist society where vested interests would always prove too strongly entrenched to permit change. Though withdrawing from party politics, he continued to use the press to publicise his views, on not only British but American economic policy. His major initiative in these years was the publication of *The Means to Prosperity* (1933) on both sides of the Atlantic. Nor was this simply a recapitulation of his old common-sense arguments for government intervention to counteract the Depression: it contained crucial new arguments, derived from his own academic work. He was in fact devoting a significant amount of his time to the composition of the *General Theory*: not published until 1936, meanwhile requiring much attention in exposition, but a work already informing his policy recommendations.

Keynes had not withdrawn to an ivory tower in Cambridge. He explained himself to Bernard Shaw on New Year's Day 1935 in a remarkable letter, infused with a sense of the dramatic that the old playwright, his ideological sparring partner, was well placed to appreciate. Enough of Marx, Keynes was saying impatiently: 'To understand my state of mind, however, you have to know that I believe myself to be writing a book on economic theory, which will largely revolutionise – not, I suppose, at once but in the course of the next ten years – the way that the world thinks about economic problems.' This in itself was a hugely ambitious claim, such as only a lunatic or a genius would make. It can be read as an early draft of the famous remarks about the influence of ideas with which the *General Theory* was to conclude. The next sentence, however, offered Shaw a hint about the complex ideological process involved: 'When my new theory has been duly assimilated and mixed with politics and feelings and passions, I can't predict what the final upshot will be in its effects on action and affairs.'[41]

Never did Keynes write truer words than these. His ideas were to achieve the extraordinary impact that he envisaged; and they were to do so through an admixture of politics and passions that he equally foresaw; and the upshot was indeed fraught with unpredictability. Two things stand out. One is that, however attached he was to the method of rational persuasion, he had few illusions about the bloodless triumph of ideas as such. The other is that he invested all the resources of his intellect, and as much of his time and energy as he could spare, in the making of the *General Theory*: a concentrated assault on inside opinion as the necessary prelude to converting outside opinion. The first words of the preface are: 'This book is addressed to my fellow economists. I hope that it will be intelligible to others.'[42]

In 1936 Keynes was at the height of his powers. The Arts Theatre was now open, the *General Theory* published, his personal fortune at a peak. He was like his own luxury motor car – he had bought a Rolls-Royce from the textile millionaire Samuel Courtauld – purring over on at least six cylinders without apparent strain. Then, at the age of fifty-three, his health started to give serious problems which he never entirely escaped. The symptoms were breathlessness and chest pains, pointing towards heart trouble. In the spring of 1937 he collapsed and needed months of recuperation.

The problem had been lurking since 1931. It seems that a bacterial infection affecting his heart was at the root of it; and that before the development of antibiotics there was no really effective treatment. It was not genetic; other members of his family had notable longevity. His heart was damaged and though he sought the best advice, orthodox and unorthodox alike, the only way he could survive was by pacing himself carefully. He was to be intermittently on the point of collapse several times, though also intermittently in periods of amazing remission in his stamina. Overwork was not really the cause but it would certainly imperil any recovery. He had to give up some of his activities, notably his chairmanship of the National Mutual, but most he contrived to retain. The only way he kept going was by being nursed through his commitments. Lydia did the nursing. Simply keeping Maynard going was to be her main task over the next nine years, in peace and war.

The First World War had posed moral dilemmas for Bloomsbury; but the Second World War, when it finally came, did not. E. M. Forster, for example, who had celebrated the values of his unlikely pacifist hero in *A Room with a View*, made it clear that the war against fascism was another matter. This was a war of conviction, then, for Keynes. Like Leonard Woolf, he had no doubts about the need to fight Hitler – whatever the costs, which had an ineluctable personal dimension. Tragically, Virginia Woolf was to find the stress too much for her, with the return of the mental afflictions which, with Leonard's constant help, she had long combated. 'The two of them were our dearest friends,' Maynard wrote in reporting Virginia's suicide to his mother in March 1941.[43]

Keynes himself had a good war. He was helped by the fact that the Second World War changed the political landscape, and made watertight party distinctions more permeable. Even in the early months, following Britain's declaration of war on Germany in September 1939, a new mood was apparent, heralding more profound dissatisfaction with the Chamberlain regime. One minor political repercussion faced Keynes, by now out of his convalescence, with a major decision about his own career.

In those days, it was an antique provision of the British constitution that the two ancient English universities, Oxford and

Lydia nurses Maynard back to an active life
after his major illness in the late 1930s.

Cambridge, each elected its own two MPs. The Labour candidate for Cambridge University in the 1935 general election, Professor Lionel Elvin, remained proud throughout a long life to have had the support of Keynes; though Elvin was ruefully resigned all along to the fact that it would do no good – two Conservatives were returned, as usual. But by the end of 1939 one of the sitting Tories had become a very sick man, which prompted thoughts of a by-election, and the Master of Magdalene College, as head of the University Conservative Committee, approached the bursar of King's – now a relatively less sick man – to see if he would accept nomination. Election was virtually automatic since all three parties agreed to support Keynes's candidature, offering him a free hand to sit as an independent.

If ever there was an opportunity for Keynes to enter the House of Commons on his own terms, this was it. He agonised over it; his doctor was unexpectedly complaisant about the idea; the Master of Magdalene was accommodating about the duties expected of an MP under the circumstances; but in the end he received a polite rejection of his proposal. 'The active political life is not my right and true activity,' Keynes told him. 'I am indeed an extremely active publicist. And that is just the difficulty.'[44] He wanted to retain not just freedom of action in parliamentary debate but freedom of action to change the terms of debate, whether by working on inside opinion or enlisting outside opinion. In short, he opted for influence over power – or perhaps achieved more power through his influence on opinion than he would have had as a backbench MP.

Keynes naturally had a plan for financing the war. Its essence was to avoid piling up debt, as in the First World War, but to mobilise the current resources of the economy – some of them currently under-employed, of course. And his plan would combat inflation, as even Hayek readily acknowledged. This particular Keynes Plan (others were to follow) was broached in three articles in *The Times* in November 1939, revised as the pamphlet 'How to Pay for the War', published in London at the end of February 1940. This was a plan for Britain but the basic idea could be applied elsewhere. Keynes finished the preface for a French edition on 4 May 1940; it was never published since the country was overrun by the Germans within weeks. But a New York edition duly appeared and was followed, later in the summer, by an article, 'The United States and the Keynes Plan', in the *New Republic* magazine, applying the author's analysis to American conditions.

The crisis of 1940 brought Churchill to power in Britain at the head of a coalition that now included Labour and the Liberals. Keynes henceforth had the satisfaction of seeing his ideas taken up by government in a way that contrasted with the complacent Conservatism of the Neville Chamberlain era. The paradox was that his most intractable challenge in persuasion was now to convince the Labour movement that his proposals were fair.

In the United States, too, he was working with the grain. The New Deal, of course, had already shown a can-do mindset that Keynes commended. The Roosevelt administration proved hospitable to his thinking when faced with the problem of mobilisation – not mobilisation for war until December 1941, as it turned out, but to serve as what the President called 'the arsenal of democracy'. Within months, government spending was to soar and unemployment to plummet. It was in his *New Republic* article on the Keynes Plan in July 1940 that its author offered the piquant comment: 'It is, it seems, politically impossible for a capitalistic democracy to organize expenditure on the scale necessary to make the grand experiments which would prove my case – except in war conditions.'[45]

The major political shift, once Churchill replaced Chamberlain, unlocked the doors of Whitehall for Keynes. In August 1940 he was given a room in the Treasury. He explained to the Provost of King's that he had 'a sort of roving commission plus membership of various high-up committees which allow me to butt in in almost any direction where I think I have something to say'.[46] That meant most directions in practice: domestic war finance entailed fiscal policy, which entailed employment issues, which entailed social policy too; and external war finance entailed foreign exchange, which entailed trade policy, which entailed imperial preference, which entailed, above all, resolving Anglo-American relations.

The Treasury soon found that it could hardly manage without its prestigious, anomalous, unique recruit. From January 1941 Keynes was formally Economic Adviser to the Chancellor of the Exchequer. Eight months later he was appointed a director of the Bank of England. Thus the former thorn in the side of 'the authorities', the man who had mocked Treasury caution and Bank inertia alike, had now been admitted into the inner sanctum. Again, the parallel with Winston Churchill's turn in fortune when his country really needed him is irresistible.

Keynes thus achieved a remarkable measure of recognition, and not just as a clever economist. He became a trustee of the National Gallery; declined a similar offer from the Tate Gallery; became chairman of the Council for the Encouragement of Music and the Arts, which later transmuted, under his active guidance, into the Arts Council. In June 1942 he accepted a peerage and sat in the House of Lords as Lord Keynes of Tilton. This pleased everyone, not least some of his old Bloomsbury friends because of the perverse satisfaction it gave them. 'O-ah!' exclaimed Lydia when they went to Charleston, 'we have come to be mocked.'[47]

Thus Keynes's long love-hate relationship with the British Treasury, and with the British establishment, found its final equipoise. Who had taken over whom? Who had taken in whom? Sir Richard Hopkins, the most formidable of the Treasury civil servants with whom Keynes had tussled for the past ten or fifteen years, easily settled into a working partnership with him, in which wary mutual respect grew into genuine warmth of esteem. Each learned from the other, with Keynes becoming more cognizant of practical administrative constraints and Hopkins more open to recasting the conventional beliefs on which he had hitherto founded his career. Likewise, Keynes even stopped snubbing the Liberal Party and sat as a Liberal in the House of Lords. He spoke there sparingly, juggling in his own mind his responsibilities at the Treasury and his desire to promote the causes in which he believed. Whenever he spoke, the impact was palpable. It was in these years that his personal influence reached its apogee.

Keynes, it seemed by 1941, was surely just the man to send to Washington, DC, armed only with his eloquence about Britain's plight and, of course, a begging bowl. He was known to have useful American connections, if only from previous visits to the United States, of which his first had been to represent the Treasury during the First World War. Maynard had returned with Lydia in 1931, and without her in 1934, the occasion of his first meeting with President Roosevelt. By 1941, when they set off on a circuitous wartime journey by flying boat, there was no question of Maynard going without Lydia; they ended up staying for three months. Together they were to make five subsequent trips: in 1943 for trade discussions; twice in 1944, first for the Bretton Woods international monetary conference and later for Lend-Lease talks; in 1945 for the postwar loan negotiations; and finally in early 1946 – a journey that an exhausted man should never have made – to the inaugural meetings of the World Bank and the International Monetary Fund.

In the United States the Keyneses lived well, temporarily spared from the privations of war-starved Britain. On three occasions they steamed out in style in the *Queen Mary*, the pride of the British passenger fleet, capable of outpacing German U-boats. On the 1943 visit, when the delegation was formally headed by the Foreign Office minister Richard Law, the economist James Meade vividly recalled Lord and Lady Keynes sweeping off the *Queen Mary* at the front of the British party in New York, to be greeted by the exploding flashbulbs of the waiting photographers – while the minister modestly shrugged his shoulders in the background. In the Pullman car of the train to Washington, DC, they engaged in 'a tremendous discussion on modern painting; and the whole journey was rounded off by Lydia singing the Casse-Noisette music at the top of her voice and dancing it with her hands'. Meade commented in his diary: 'We had been instructed to slip into Washington unnoticed: as far as the Keynes party was concerned, I do not think that we attained our objective.'[48]

We cannot know how many Americans innocently formed their impressions of typical British behaviour and temperament from such displays. Lydia shopped till she dropped on more than one well-remembered occasion; and, when she came back to their hotel suite to show off her prizes, Maynard would happily break off discussions with colleagues and instead get them to marvel at her splendid purchases (many of them for friends in England). But the foreign currency needed to finance her visits was well spent; she earned her rewards if only by keeping Maynard alive.

The demands made upon him had unpredictable effects upon his health. Sometimes he was buoyed up by the challenges he faced; sometimes floored by the sapping effect of long sessions with endlessly loquacious Americans who felt the lash of his tongue. The number of legal experts who were brought into the negotiations baffled Keynes, who speculated that the *Mayflower* must have been full of lawyers. In particular, he could not bear the legalese in which, it seemed, the United States like to wrap its business, and called it 'Cherokee'. Obviously this was not particularly tactful, or politically correct, but people spoke differently in those days. Keynes undoubtedly meant it as a compliment when he reported home from Washington that 'the younger Civil Servants and advisers strike me as exceptionally capable and vigorous (with the very gritty Jewish type perhaps a little too prominent)'.[49] This was the same Keynes who had made vigorous efforts to help many Jewish friends and colleagues escape either discriminatory treatment or even internment as aliens – a man of parts in all sorts of ways.

Keynes was thus the best and the worst person for negotiation with the Americans. He mastered the whole brief on Lend-Lease: the simple idea with which Roosevelt solved the problem of how to keep Britain in the war once its own financial reserves were exhausted by 1941. But this simple root had proliferated dense and impenetrable foliage. When put into proper contractual form, the agreements were replete with terminology that was never meant to bear only a single, clear, unambiguous interpretation. Two countries were indeed divided by a common language. They were divided, too, by divergent war aims, especially over whether this was a war to avert what Churchill called 'the liquidation of the British Empire'.[50] And they were divided by different political traditions, which Keynes first misapprehended himself and then tried unavailingly to convey to his masters in Whitehall. Such differences between British and American practice were to have profound effects on the contrasting reception and application of his own economic ideas in the two countries, as will be seen in the epilogue.

The British constitutional model, on which Keynes had been brought up, was that of a unitary executive. If backed by a stable parliamentary majority, this guaranteed acceptance of whatever was agreed by ministers; and the civil servants knew this. In practice, the Treasury co-ordinated the system, which relied on meticulous preparation of briefs, cleared in advance and thereafter accepted as policy by all British officials, high and low alike. Keynes had often hated the way that Whitehall would close ranks against him; but as long as he sat in the driving seat in the Treasury, he loved it. These were the rules of a game that he had learned to play, to play well, and to play for keeps.

What Keynes found in Washington, however, was truly something else. The American model seemed to be all over the place, with different agencies competing against each other, refusing to fall into line, reaching understandings with the British on a verbal basis that might subsequently be repudiated when the wind changed, and were in any case subject to the whims of what happened on Capitol Hill, where the fluctuations of public opinion could apparently send everyone back to the drawing board. It is not quite true to say that Keynes despaired of this way of doing business, since he also sought to exploit it.

One result was double-edged for the British. In several important sets of international negotiations, despite their inferior numbers and wealth, they began better prepared than the Americans through prior staffwork (which only the Canadians matched). This was, on the face of it, an advantage since it set the Americans scrambling to improvise their own response as they went along. But it also became a disadvantage for the British, who were perceived as seizing an unfair advantage in conspiring between themselves in this underhand way. Moreover in the press – and everything seemed to get into the American press – the stereotypes were of simple, honest Yanks being duped by clever, wily Limeys. Among the latter, the name of Lord Keynes stood high.

Here was an explosive mixture. Clashes of interest and ideology between Britain and the United States were compounded by clashes of method and personality too. Moreover, the bottom line was always the sheer preponderant power of the United States, which gave its representatives a muscle for which Keynes's quick brain could not compensate. In the protracted negotiations that culminated at Bretton Woods in 1944, Keynes faced the influential American Treasury official Harry Dexter White (whom we now know to have been passing information to the Soviet Union). Two of Keynes's younger colleagues, the distinguished economists Lionel Robbins and James Meade, both kept diaries, which mixed admiration for Keynes with apprehension about how far he would go. Admittedly, White was fully able to hold his own in this histrionic league over issues of interpretation. 'This is intolerable,' Keynes cried at one point. 'It is yet another Talmud. We had better simply break off negotiations.' Then White replied: 'We will try to produce something which your Highness can understand.' Meade wrote sadly of his hero Keynes: 'That man is a menace in international relations.'[51]

Yet it was Keynes who did the necessary deal with White to produce the Bretton Woods agreements. In 1943 a new Keynes Plan, this time for the postwar international monetary system, had been published, promising an escape from the bad old days of the Gold Standard. Keynes had been working on his ideas for a clearing union since the end of 1940, initially to counter the appeal of Hitler's 'New Order'. Confronted with this sort of alternative, Keynes needed little prompting to look instead to Anglo-American co-operation in reviving a liberal trading system.

What had changed Keynes's mind was the changed American attitude under the Roosevelt regime. Back in the 1920s, drafting *A Tract on Monetary Reform*, he had written: 'Much as I admire the Americans, when *laissez-faire* takes the form of agreeing to do whatever the Americans do, I am a little terrified.'[52] But this was in the era of the Gold Standard, which Britain had been forced to abandon in 1931 and which Roosevelt had repudiated in 1933. There was ample room for Anglo-American co-operation in devising an international monetary system along lines that would promote rather than undermine full employment. But this would only be acceptable to the Americans alongside a new international trade system.

Everyone agreed by now that the protectionist measures adopted in the 1930s had proved collectively self-defeating. Keynes thus rediscovered the virtues of Free Trade all over again; or perhaps saw how a more equitable model of Free Trade might be instituted for the postwar world. In principle, trade and currency issues could be separated; in practice they could not, if only because the Americans insisted on it. And what riled them was not tariffs as such (which the United States had long imposed) but the sort of tariffs that discriminated between different trading partners – in short, exactly the sort of preferential tariffs that had been implemented since 1932 between members of the British Empire and Commonwealth. The British saw clearly how hypocritical the Americans were in wanting to dismantle imperial preference while keeping their own tariffs; and the Americans were equally perceptive in seeing the British hypocrisy in commending moves towards Free Trade while clinging to preference. Such conflicts impinged on efforts to reform the currency system.

The Keynes Plan was characteristically bold. Rather than tying currencies to gold, Keynes wanted to invent a new international medium of exchange. The name he preferred, 'Bancor', is a pun that works better in French – literally 'bank gold', which would substitute for the precious metal itself in lubricating international transactions. Created out of thin air by an effort of will, Bancor need never be in short supply like gold but would, in effect, give each country an overdraft facility for financing its own trade. It would provide the necessary international liquidity. Thus full employment could be maintained by escaping the deflationary pressures endemic under the Gold Standard.

This Keynes Plan was an elegant conception, which even White claimed privately to like. But the alternative White Plan, simultaneously published, was bound to triumph at the time, since it mobilised American support for a less visionary alternative, more consistent alike with good old-fashioned banking principles and populist sentiments. As one Iowa newspaper saw it: 'If we are big enough suckers to swallow the Keynes plan, we shall be swindled out of everything we have left from the war – and we shall deserve to be swindled.'[53]

Hence the need for Keynes to compromise, which he did. The problem was to create a new international structure for both trade and the flows of currency to finance it; and whatever was put forward simply had to have the support not only of the US government but of American public opinion, as Keynes came to appreciate. By the time of the Bretton Woods international conference in 1944, he had thrown his weight behind a reformulated White Plan that broke with the Gold Standard and made the International Monetary Fund (IMF) the custodian of a financial system based on fixed but adjustable exchange rates, pegged to the US dollar. A parallel institution, called the World Bank, would be set up, responsible for development. It did not escape comment that the fund was thus really a bank, whereas the bank was really a fund. All this was agreed by the international conference at Bretton Woods in July 1944.

Further Anglo-American negotiations later that year saw Keynes again in top form. 'Maynard's performance was truly wonderful,' reported one British civil servant, adding that 'the impression which he makes on the Americans gives us an enormous initial advantage in any negotiations on which he participates. Take Harry White, for instance – that difficult nature unfolds like a flower when Maynard is there, and he is quite different to deal with when under the spell than he is in our normal day to day relations with him.'[54] Like Churchill, Keynes had a special touch in fostering the affinities between the English-speaking peoples. Like Churchill, he naturally exploited such rhetorical appeals in the British national interest. Like Churchill too, he may have swallowed some of his own propaganda in overestimating the British role in any postwar Anglo-American relationship.

The inaugural meetings of the World Bank and the International Monetary Fund were to take place at Savannah, Georgia, in March 1946. By then Keynes had been appointed as the British governor of the two institutions and looked forward to attending.

The actual meetings were somewhat disappointing; Keynes did not take it as a good sign that the Americans insisted on the new institutions being sited in Washington rather than New York, near the United Nations. As usual, however, he made the best of things, hoping that the good fairies would prevail.

Bancor thus passed into history. It could be dismissed as one of the bright ideas that passed through the busy mind of John Maynard Keynes, only to prove impracticable under real-world conditions. For the Bretton Woods system was indeed, for a quarter of a century, to be based upon the hegemony of the US dollar; and the latter survived the former, despite President Nixon's decision to suspend the dollar's convertibility with gold in 1971. Thus it seemed merely a fact of life that the dollar should reign supreme as an international reserve currency, with the IMF and its 'special drawing rights' (SDRs) effectively subservient to it. Yet in March 2009 the governor of China's central bank, with an authority reinforced by current American problems, launched a proposal for the IMF to replace the dollar by expanding the role of SDRs into a new international reserve currency. In doing so, with proper respect for the ancestors, he acknowledged a debt to Keynes.[55]

In 1945 Keynes endured the last of his arduous Anglo-American negotiations. He was sent to Washington within a couple of weeks of the end of the Second World War. As usual, the British were asking for more dollars. This time their story was that they were broke but that somehow it was the Americans' responsibility to bail them out. Whoever had come up with that line? And whoever was going to persuade the Americans to go along with it?

The answer to both questions, of course, was Lord Keynes. He had long foreseen that overwhelming financial difficulties would face Britain as soon as Lend-Lease came to an end. For Lend-Lease had distorted the whole shape of the British economy, replacing its own manufacturing capacity with American production, free of charge, so as to maximise Britain's military contribution to the Allied war effort. This was, of course, generous on the part of the Americans, who could afford such generosity precisely because their own industries were booming, likewise to feed the Allied war effort.

It was a benign model of Keynesian synergy, at any rate for the duration of hostilities – which suddenly ended after the atomic bombs took Japan out of the war in August 1945. It seemed obvious in Washington that Lend-Lease must cease, virtually overnight. It seemed obvious in London that the British economy could not snap back into its peacetime shape, virtually overnight. Keynes had long since warned the Treasury that, unless agreement had meanwhile been reached with the United States, the situation would be 'awkward'.[56]

It was. Keynes knew that he would be faced with 'the toughest mission yet' when he reached Washington in early September.[57] Flanked by Lord Halifax, the elegantly aristocratic British ambassador, he began negotiations that were to last nearly three months. He had left Britain's new Labour Government probably more optimistic than he intended. 'When I listen to Lord Keynes talking, I seem to hear those coins jingling in my pocket,' said the Foreign Secretary, Ernest Bevin; 'but I am not so sure that they are really there.'[58] For Keynes had persuaded them, and persuaded himself, that he was simply asking for 'Justice', which was hardly something that the good-natured Americans were likely to repudiate. Justice demanded that the costs of fighting in the common cause be equitably shared – costs that had bankrupted Britain in standing alone during the two years before American intervention. So what Keynes was really suggesting was that a sort of retrospective Lend-Lease windfall was morally due to Britain. In London, nearly everyone readily agreed with him.

Not so in Washington. It seemed outrageous that the British, who had so long been supported by US dollars, should now be asking for more by implying that the United States had been remiss in not entering the war until after Pearl Harbor. Keynes's learning curve chiefly educated him about the distance between London and Washington. As usual he learned quickly and was soon lecturing the government back in London about the futility of simply asking for a gift-in-aid of the sort he had recently convinced them might be forthcoming. In the end he had to settle instead for a loan, probably less in amount than if he had asked for it in the first place, and bearing interest, of course. The level of interest was set ridiculously low in American eyes, but the fact that it was demanded at all was humiliating in British eyes.

All Keynes's cleverness could not change these realities. A piece of doggerel, found on a scrap of paper that survives from the period, still captures a truth that can be read as a satire on either the bumptious Americans or the supercilious British:[59]

> In Washington Lord Halifax
> Once whispered to Lord Keynes:
> 'It's true *they* have the money bags
> But we have all the brains.'

Keynes saw the postwar dollar loan as vital. It underpinned Britain's ability to survive an orderly transition from the command economy of wartime, sustained externally by Lend-Lease, to economic viability within a liberal international trading and currency system. This, of course, was the vision of Bretton Woods, which he had played a conspicuous role in bringing forward. Once the maintenance of full employment had been built into this scheme as a desirable objective, Keynes's objections to Free Trade were allayed, though not his fears about the free movement of capital.

Keynes tried to square the circle on his return from Washington to the very different climate of London. The deadline for ratification of the Bretton Woods agreements was 31 December 1945 and essentially Parliament had to accept the terms of the loan first. So if the loan went down, so did British participation in the Bretton Woods system of liberal international trading arrangements. There were two alternatives to acceptance, each ideologically charged. But neither the left-wingers' command economy nor the right-wingers' imperial protectionism appealed to Keynes. So acquiescence was necessary, on the Americans' terms, the only terms available. This was the gist of one of the most important speeches of his life, addressing an attentive and deeply troubled audience in the House of Lords, which needed to consent.

The huge problem in persuasion that Keynes now faced was partly of his own making. He had pumped up the rhetoric of 'Justice', talked up the chances of getting it, written off any fall-back option as defeatist; yet now he had to persuade those of his compatriots who had trustingly gone along with his scenario that they needed to sign up none the less. The thrust of his speech – 'I give the American point of view' – was partly to put forward arguments he had just spent three months contesting.

The bigger point was that the loan was a means to an end: a revival of hope for international trade as the true means to prosperity. The protectionism of the 1930s may have seemed inevitable in its day but had proved barren in its results. Keynes had long since ceased to be a dogmatic free-trader of the old school. But he remained consistent in his confidence in a reformed free-market system when he commended 'an attempt to use what we have learnt from modern experience and modern analysis, not to defeat, but to implement the wisdom of Adam Smith'.[60]

The House of Commons had already accepted the loan by 345 to 98 and Bretton Woods by 314 to 50. Winston Churchill had got most of the Conservatives to abstain, thus muffling opposition from the elected representatives; but the real trouble was expected from rebel Conservatives in the Lords, where party discipline was weaker. In the event, however, the loan was approved by 90 to 8, with many abstentions. Keynes's intervention was widely credited with doing the trick. It was to be his last speech in the House of Lords.

Keynes was determined to go to Savannah, to see the Bretton Woods institutions launched, at the end of March 1946. But on his return to Britain his health was a recurrent worry. He went to Tilton to rest over the Easter holidays. He was driven twice that week on the military road that winds up Firle Beacon. This hill is one of the highest points on the South Downs, at about 700 feet (210 metres). But it seems higher because of its dramatically steep chalk escarpment which, on a fine Easter day, gives an unobstructed view from the top, beyond Tilton House and Charleston, across the Sussex Weald far below, now largely farmland but covered in previous centuries by thick forest. Even further back in time, the top of the Downs was a safe retreat, testified by the visible archaeological remains, for ancient settlement – by people whose ideas of money were certainly very different from our own. Yet it was Keynes's *A Treatise on Money* that had expressed the caution: 'Money, like other essential elements in civilisation, is a far more ancient institution than we were taught to believe some few years ago.'[61]

Maynard asked to be driven to the top of Firle Beacon for a third visit on Saturday 20 April 1946. He felt well enough to walk down with Lydia to their home, nestled below, sending his octogenarian mother ahead in the car. But the next morning, Easter Sunday, Maynard suffered a further heart attack. Both Lydia and Florence Keynes were with him when he died. His father was to live to ninety-seven, his mother to ninety-six, his brother to ninety-five, his widow to eighty-eight; so Maynard Keynes might well have been expected to live into the 1960s or

1970s and participate in ongoing arguments about his work. As it was, he died a few weeks short of his sixty-third birthday – a full life in which he liked to claim that his only serious regret was not having drunk more champagne.

3

'In the long run we are all dead'
Rethinking economic policy

THROUGHOUT HIS LIFE, Keynes refused to compart-
mentalise his activities. It was the same man with the
same active mind who turned – sometimes with dazzling and
disconcerting speed – from books to the ballet, from mathematics
to morality, from intellectual speculation to the financial kind, from
rarefied economic theory to immediate practical policy (and back
again). It is, admittedly, as an economist that he achieved greatness,
and as an economist that his ideas retain their abiding interest. But
his thinking should not be reduced to a simple formula – least of
all a mathematical formula – with the label 'Keynesianism' stuck
to it. For one thing, he changed his mind too often to make such
doctrinal distillation profitable, though it is obviously reasonable
to suppose that he regarded his later ideas as superior to those that
he had meanwhile discarded.

Such qualifications aside, it does make sense to speak of a
Keynesian approach to economic problems. At least from 1924,
Keynes's economic thinking exhibits a measure of consistency in
policy terms; and, as early as 1932, he was seized of a vision with
more fundamental implications for economic theory. This is what
justifies us, in this chapter and the next, in exploring two stages
of a process of rethinking the orthodoxies of the day, first with an

emphasis on Keynesian economic policy and then on Keynesian economic theory.

Before there was Keynesianism or Keynesians, there was the historical Keynes: the man whom his contemporaries knew. His biographer raised one question that is surely worth attention, prompted by Keynes's noteworthy last speech in the House of Lords in December 1945. 'The speech was indeed an excellent one, compounded of penetrating analysis, tact and sagacity,' commented Harrod, unsurprisingly. 'But Keynes had been talking in this style about matters of grave importance to the well-being of the country for some twenty-seven years. Why had his words not been listened to with equal respect during all this long period?'[1]

Harrod's question provokes others, which this chapter and the next will address. How exactly did Keynes himself, in his own lifetime, argue his case? How much can be recaptured, not just of what he conveyed on the printed page, but of how he exercised his personal influence over his own contemporaries? This may help us to understand how persuasive he seemed at the time (rightly or not) to those he succeeded in winning over; and, equally important, how unpersuasive he seemed to those who (rightly or not) could not stand him or his proposals. We can try to assess how far his arguments were specific to his own time and place – or how far they still have relevance for us today.

Many of Keynes's friends and colleagues were themselves remarkable people. Virtually all of them, however eminent in their own fields, readily acknowledged his almost uncanny powers of argument and hence of persuasion. 'When I argued with him, I felt that I took my life in my hands, and I seldom emerged without feeling something of a fool,' wrote one.[2] This was the intellectually formidable philosopher Bertrand Russell, eleven years older than Keynes. A similar sense of awe is conveyed by another academic titan of the next generation, Lionel Robbins, fifteen years younger than Keynes, who had fiercely argued with him over pre-war economic policy but became a close wartime colleague. Robbins left in his diary a memorable vignette of Keynes in action, speaking to a joint Anglo-American session at the Bretton Woods conference.

> At such moments, I often find myself thinking that Keynes must be one of the most remarkable men that have ever lived – the quick logic, the birdlike swoop of intuition, the vivid fancy, the wide vision, above all the incomparable sense of the fitness of words, all combine to make something several degrees beyond the limit of ordinary human achievement ... He uses the classical style of our life and language, it is true, but it is shot through with something which is not traditional, a unique unearthly quality of which one can only say that it is pure genius. The Americans sat entranced as the God-like visitor sang and the golden light played around.[3]

Such magic can be potent but ephemeral. The spell that is cast may not last very long, especially not outlast the death of the spellbinder. How much did Keynes's influence owe to his own charismatic powers? How far might his own death be expected to diminish the influence of the ideas that he left behind? Alternatively, why has the influence of Keynes's ideas so resiliently survived his own death, more than sixty years ago?

There are many places that one might look for answers. But one source is so compelling in its verisimilitude that it repays particularly close scrutiny, despite its chronologically limited scope. For we are lucky to have an almost verbatim record of Keynes expounding his current ideas for an intelligent lay audience, and doing so at a critical moment. This came about because, in the autumn of 1929, an official committee was set up by the minority Labour Government to report on finance and industry, with official stenographers transcribing every word over the course of more than twelve months. Here we can catch Keynes in motion,

in action, and in earnest, seeking to persuade others of the validity
of his analysis of deep-seated problems that stretched back into the
1920s and that looked ahead into the 1930s. We are surely justified
in dwelling on this uniquely well-documented episode for what it
can disclose more generally about the course of his thinking about
economic policy.

In 1929 Britain's existing economic troubles were both paralleled
and exacerbated by the dramatic crash of share prices on Wall
Street – October seems to be the cruellest month in such matters.
The crisis was not helped when the Republican President Hoover
was prodded into declaring that 'the fundamental business of the
country, that is production and distribution of commodities, is on
a sound and prosperous basis'.[4]

This was the context for the appointment in Britain of the
Committee on Finance and Industry, under the chairmanship
of a judge, Lord Macmillan. The Chancellor of the Exchequer
later explained that it had been set up 'largely because of the
impression made on public opinion by Mr Keynes's proposals'
and the Treasury came round under the pressure of events to
accepting that, if it had to put 'an economist of the Keynes school'
on the Macmillan committee, this single, token, isolated, marginal,
maverick member might as well be Keynes himself.[5]

To the alarm of 'the authorities', Keynes quickly succeeded in
taking charge of the committee's agenda, as the day-by-day, line-
by-line record shows. It was important that he found two powerful
allies among the other members. One was Reginald McKenna, a
former Chancellor of the Exchequer under Asquith, and now,
as head of the Midland Bank, Britain's biggest high-street bank,
already a critic of Bank of England orthodoxy. The other was the
massive figure of Ernest Bevin, the undisputed boss of Britain's
biggest trade union, which he was largely responsible for creating:
a self-taught man who had set out to master economics with the

innate self-confidence and intuitive common sense with which he was later to set out to master international affairs as Foreign Secretary. With both his old patron McKenna and his new sympathiser Bevin, Keynes enjoyed productive relationships based on mutual respect for the diverse experience that each of them brought to the table.

Keynes did not come to this table unprepared. He came to do battle for the ideas that he had been formulating for several years. These took the form of proposals to tackle the high postwar level of unemployment by applying 'the stimulus which shall initiate a cumulative prosperity'.[6] Specifically, in the general election of May 1929, the plans in the pamphlet that he and Hubert Henderson wrote, 'Can Lloyd George Do It?', were central. They aimed at cutting British unemployment (currently 1.14 million) by creating half a million jobs through loan expenditure of £100 million (perhaps to be continued for two further years). To put these figures in perspective, the total size of the budget at this time was about £800 million or, as we now calculate it, 20 per cent of Gross Domestic Product (GDP). As Keynes correctly guessed (in the absence of official statistics), £100 million was about 2.5 per cent of national income (roughly corresponding to GDP). This compares with a discretionary fiscal stimulus, as calculated for most G20 countries in 2009, in the range of 1–2 per cent of GDP, with the United States at the high end, Canada and Germany just above average and the United Kingdom just below.[7]

Keynes did not put this forward as the ideal policy. He was not a socialist; he did not believe in a command economy; he had no doctrinaire reason to advocate state intervention; his whole education as an economist taught him that it was generally best to leave things to be sorted out by the free play of market forces. But what if the market seemed to be failing to perform as the textbooks prescribed? What was the best option under such conditions? The orthodox answer was to show patience. Keynes's answer was to opt for second-best expedients.

Here is an issue at the nub of the whole debate about Keynesian economic policy. The key text is the one that is so often cited by hostile critics, selectively quoting Keynes's *A Tract on Monetary Reform* (1923). This was published well before Britain went back on the Gold Standard, at a time when its author was a loyal follower of Marshall in economic theory and a dutiful adherent of the axiomatic canons of Free Trade. Yet when the *Tract* dealt with the quantity theory of money (which had so taxed Lydia) it did not stop with its flat endorsement of the theory itself: 'Its correspondence with fact is not open to question.'[8] Instead, Keynes went on to explore what was meant by the doctrine that a change in the quantity of currency in circulation would ultimately have no effect upon the quantity of consumption, since money prices would simply adjust. 'Now, "in the long run" this is probably true,' Keynes conceded, before briskly commenting: 'But this *long run* is a misleading guide to current affairs. *In the long run* we are all dead. Economists set themselves too easy, too useless a task if in tempestuous seasons they can only tell us that when the storm is long past the ocean is flat again.'[9]

Joseph Schumpeter made a memorable comment on this aphorism of his great rival: 'He was childless and his philosophy of life was essentially a short-run philosophy.'[10] Perhaps there is a homophobic sub-text here; but even if the remark is regarded as simply ignorant, it is obviously personally inappropriate to Keynes, who wanted children of his own and took the needs of notional grandchildren as the criterion of good economic policy. It is surely Schumpeter who comes out worse in the long run. We can now see that, as an economist of conservative inclinations, he refused to accept that there was anything much to be done by government when faced with the slump. He preferred to repose confidence in an ultimately benign process of 'creative destruction', a Schumpeterian vision that has (quite rightly) informed our understanding of the dynamics of modern capitalism.

In the Keynesian vision, however, such inaction is itself irresponsible. It may be that the author of the *Treatise on Probability* remembered its argument that our powers of prediction are so fallible, and our immunity from unintended consequences so frail, that it is simply not prudent to look too far ahead. Under such circumstances, it may be rational to base our actions on a relatively short run over which we have more control. But the fundamental point is surely that the best can be the enemy of the good.

Keynes laid down a basic principle as early as the *Tract*: 'When, therefore, we enter the realm of State action, *everything* is to be considered and weighed on its merits.'[11] And in the real world we are faced with second-best options, *all* of which may be far from ideal, but *some* of which may be better than remaining inert through misguided doctrinal purity. Our choices ought to be the best that we can make at the time, with a natural likelihood of error. Thus Keynes was to write in 1933, at the time of the abortive world economic conference and at the beginning of the New Deal: 'We do not know what will be the outcome. We are – all of us, I expect – about to make many mistakes.'[12] This was all the more reason for trying to do something, not an excuse for doing nothing.

Little wonder, then, that Keynes had emerged as the leading critic of 'the authorities' in Britain. For the Treasury and the Bank of England were united in upholding what Keynes called laissez-faire. They adhered to a deliberately non-interventionist model of the economy. Like the House of Lords – as celebrated in Gilbert and Sullivan's *Iolanthe* – they did nothing in particular, and did it very well. The Treasury doctrine, handed down since Gladstone in the late nineteenth century, was to preserve a system that was 'knave-proof', that is, immune from the base political temptations to which opportunistic politicians like Lloyd George were all too susceptible. The Treasury's role was to balance the books, as the national housekeeper, not to try to manage the economy, as the national breadwinner.

Three interlocking principles were therefore inviolable: balanced budgets, Free Trade and the Gold Standard. Each purposely restricted the initiative of government under a system that was intended to be self-acting and self-regulating. The trouble was that the First World War had simultaneously run the budget into deficit, introduced the thin end of the tariff wedge and taken Britain off gold for the duration. Hence the prime aim of the authorities to go back on to gold, which was the British version of getting back to the sort of 'normalcy' with which the Republican presidential candidate in 1920, Warren Harding, had reproached radical critics and offended linguistic pedants.

In all of this the Treasury worked hand-in-glove with the Bank of England. Its governor for a uniquely long term, from 1920 to 1944, was Montagu Norman: a remote and aloof figure, subject to neurotic breakdown, but commanding a respect bordering on mystique as the bankers' banker. The robust instincts of Winston Churchill, Chancellor of the Exchequer from 1924 to 1929, led him to question the prevailing orthodoxy. 'I would rather see Finance less proud and Industry more content,' he growled. But he buckled in face of the stern advice from Sir Otto Niemeyer (as Keynes's old rival in the Treasury had now become) about the criteria that should guide the authorities. 'The real antithesis is rather between the long view and the short view,' Niemeyer told Churchill. 'Bankers on the whole take longer views than manufacturers.'[13]

Keynes was unlikely to be persuaded by such appeals to the inherent virtues of the long run. Moreover he detected a sort of leftover Victorian piety and smugness, almost Pecksniffian, for which Bloomsbury had no time. Keynes had already given his own opinion in the *Tract* that 'many conservative bankers regard it as more consonant with their cloth, and also as economising thought, to shift public discussion of financial topics off the logical on to an alleged "moral" plane, which means a realm of thought where vested interest can be triumphant over the common good without further debate'.[14] But, argue as he might, the authorities remained united in telling Churchill that he had to go back to gold in 1925. 'The Gold Standard,' Norman confidently claimed, 'is the best "Governor" that can be devised for a world that is still human, rather than divine.'[15]

It was natural that the Macmillan committee should begin its work by summoning the governor of the Bank of England as its first witness in November 1929. Characteristically at such a moment of stress, Norman took to his bed, sent his deputy and did not appear in person until four months later. Meanwhile this delay gave Keynes his chance to educate the committee, notably in a series of five sessions of 'private evidence' in which he expounded his own thinking. He conducted these meetings with his customary aplomb, virtually as a seminar.

In doing so he was singularly well prepared. Through fortuitous timing, he was able to expound the themes of his new book, eventually published in October 1930 as *A Treatise on Money*, in two volumes totalling over 700 pages. Dealing with both the pure and the applied theory of money, this was the big academic book that was needed to establish his professional credentials. Schumpeter wrote with congratulations on the completion of a work that he looked forward to reading. But how many members of the Macmillan committee would have said the same? 'I have written this out at great length in technical language,' Keynes told them in February 1930, before offering them, in effect, a beginners' guide to the *Treatise*.[16]

The book's philosophy can be seen from a passage added at a late stage. 'It has been usual to think of the accumulated wealth of the world as having been painfully built up out of that voluntary abstinence of individuals from the immediate enjoyment of consumption which we call thrift,' it claims. 'But it should be obvious that mere abstinence is not enough by itself to build cities or drain fens.' This no doubt seemed a sensible observation in Cambridge, a city built by draining a fen. So what had actually done the trick and created the wealth of nations? 'It is enterprise which builds and improves the world's possessions,' the *Treatise* tells us, with a rhetoric that loads the terms to suit the dynamics of the analysis. 'If enterprise is afoot, wealth accumulates whatever may be happening to thrift; and if enterprise is asleep, wealth decays whatever thrift may be doing.'[17]

The chapter on historical illustrations, from which this is quoted, challenges the conventional values of its day. At the time, saving remained prized and honoured as the key to economic recovery. Keynes's serious point is to distinguish saving (or thrift), which is essentially negative, from the real motor of economic growth, investment (or enterprise). This is why thrift is out, and with it the conventional bankers' resort to deflation in times of crisis. By the same token, it is why enterprise is in, and with it a more tolerant view of what society has owed to historical episodes of inflation. Thus England experienced 'the sensational rise of prices' of the years 1560 to 1650 with happy results – 'We were just in a financial position to afford Shakespeare at the moment when he presented himself!'[18] How different the country's more recent history, when in 1925 the return to the Gold Standard was accompanied by a credit squeeze 'with the object of producing out of the blue a cold-blooded income deflation'.[19]

Keynes sought to convey the novelty of his insights to his students on the Macmillan committee. But there was another professor at the table: Theodore Gregory of the London School of Economics (LSE), put there by the authorities as an expert on the banking system and as an obvious check on any Keynesian unorthodoxy. Gregory, however, was no doctrinaire and, content to bide his time, had a good point when he maintained that 'there is not a very wide margin of difference between him and myself on some of the analytical points he has raised'. As he said, 'I think the main difference will come over points of policy rather than over theoretical points.' It was Keynes who sought to sharpen their differences by claiming, 'I think it makes a revolution in the mind when you think clearly of the distinction between saving and investment.'[20]

The fact is that the *Treatise* was not as incompatible with orthodox economic theory as its author imagined it to be at the time. Little wonder that Schumpeter considered it Keynes's best book. Its rhetoric was challenging but its great analytical strength – as Keynes's presentation of it to the Macmillan committee brought out – was its lucid account of the mechanisms by which the monetary system was supposed to work, especially the Gold Standard. 'An extraordinarily clear exposition,' the chairman congratulated Keynes, and McKenna chipped in: 'An extraordinarily clear exposition, and thoroughly understood by us.' It was left to Gregory to add defensively: 'It may be a very beautiful and perfect series of assumptions – but they were in fact assumptions which worked.' McKenna conceded: 'Pre-War, they worked.' Gregory, civil but determined, then reiterated his point: 'I accept everything that Mr Keynes has said, but I should like to emphasise that this is not only a beautiful series of assumptions, but assumptions which translated into action have worked.'[21]

But had they worked? Did they still work? How effectively were these beautiful assumptions translated into action? Why was Finance so proud of them and Industry so discontented? These were now the key issues, with the official unemployment figures in Britain hovering around 10 per cent throughout the 1920s, averaging 16 per cent in 1930 and over 21 per cent by 1931.

Professor A. C. Pigou was Marshall's successor as Professor of Political Economy at Cambridge, thus holding the most prestigious economics chair in the country. As such, he would have his two days before the Macmillan committee in due course. Less than six years older than Keynes, he seemed already of an older generation, stiff in his manner, cautious in his scholarship. Keynes later took him as representative of the 'classical school', devoting seven pages of the *General Theory* to a demolition of Pigou's *The Theory of Unemployment* (1933). Of all the economists whom Keynes might have chosen as the straw man of orthodox economics, to be publicly knocked down, he chose Pigou, the bearer of the Marshallian flame, his colleague in the Cambridge Economics Faculty and a Fellow of King's College like Keynes himself.

It was a small world. Pigou had been more generous when he reviewed Keynes's *Treatise*, saying that it provided 'an account of the *modus operandi* of bank rate much superior, as it seems to me, to previous discussions'.[22] True enough, and from an impeccably orthodox source. For at this time Keynes's real achievement was not any theoretical innovation of his own but his lucidly cogent analysis of how the conventional theoretical mechanisms worked – or failed to work – in practice.

Many people in Britain, with the benefit of hindsight, came to agree that going back on to the Gold Standard in 1925 had not been very clever. Churchill later talked of it as 'the biggest blunder of his life'.[23] What distinguished Keynes was that he had publicly identified this policy disaster with the benefit of foresight. 'The Economic Consequences of Mr Churchill' (1925) had set out the case. He made it clear that he was not against the Gold Standard as such but 'against having restored gold in conditions which required a substantial readjustment of all our money values'. British prices would have to come down to make the pound sterling actually worth as much as $4.86 in purchasing power. So Churchill was accused of 'committing himself to force down money wages and all money values, without any idea how it was to be done. Why did he do such a silly thing?'[24]

It was essential to appreciate the process that was set in train. By what mechanism could dear money (or credit restriction) bring down real wages? *In no other way than by the deliberate intensification of unemployment.*[25] Here were the real-world consequences of the long views taken by the bankers and commended by Niemeyer and the other Treasury knights. Niemeyer had not been afraid to take a hard line that he admitted was 'necessarily put in a doctrinaire way'.[26] The return to gold might face British industry with temporary difficulties, now that exports were uncompetitive at the new exchange rate; but prices were surely flexible, were they not?

This was inescapably an issue with a social dimension. 'The gold standard, with its dependence on pure chance, its faith in "automatic adjustments", and its general regardlessness of social detail, is an essential emblem and idol of those who sit in the top tier of the machine,' wrote Keynes.[27] He had sat there himself; he knew whereof he spoke. Perhaps in our day the clever people in the top tier of the IMF, when demanding similar adjustments from developing countries, have done so with a similar blithe obliviousness of the consequences.

If Keynes spoke with less passion on this subject to the Macmillan committee in 1930, it was for a good reason. Admittedly, he always found it difficult to be dull. But he badly wanted to be listened to by the committee, not as a polemical policy advocate, but 'as a scientist' who would first identify the problem before specifying what remedies were appropriate.

The problem was that savings and investment were out of kilter. It was interest rate that had the job of bringing them into equilibrium, finding a point at which the rate was low enough to encourage investors but high enough to reward savers. In a slump, it was enterprise that needed stimulation through low interest rates, so it was reasonable to suppose that the rate of interest would always fall accordingly, since 'there are always plenty of useful things to do at a price if you can borrow cheap enough'.[28] But this was only true of a closed system, where interest rate had this flexibility. In an international system, however, interest rate had a second task – one that took priority in the eyes of the central bank. This was to maintain the value of the currency itself, by setting interest rates at a high enough level to protect the foreign exchange reserves. So a country's internal need for cheap money might be trumped by its external necessity to impose dear money.

In theory, equilibrium could still be achieved. All that was required was that domestic prices make the adjustments necessary to keep in line with international prices. This could be achieved either by a process of inflation through a low interest rate, to raise domestic prices, or by deflation through a high interest rate, to bring prices down. An inflationary adjustment presented no problem, since there would naturally be little resistance to wage increases, for example. A deflationary adjustment was more difficult, requiring painful cuts, but had proved historically feasible. Small adjustments in both directions had thus been relatively easy to make before 1914, especially for a creditor country like Britain with big reserves that could themselves absorb some of the shock. In particular, the balance of payments – like any balance sheet – could be *made* to balance, in this case through a rise or fall in the residual level of investment overseas.

In the cold, hard world of the 1920s, however, the shock-absorbers were largely absent. The wartime erosion of Britain's overseas investments was one obvious difference. Rebuilding them was now acknowledged as a strain on the balance of payments, but London's financial prestige was felt to be at stake, with its continuing pretensions to act as the world's banker. The Gold Standard was the symbol of all this; the necessity of going back on gold was the bankers' article of faith. It meant that 'the pound could look the dollar in the face', as the saying went, or that the pound would be 'as good as gold', just as it had been before 1914. 'In truth,' Keynes had whispered in the *Tract*, 'the gold standard is already a barbarous relic.'[29]

In 1925, when Churchill took his heroic step, or did 'such a silly thing', $4.86 was the only parity seriously considered. It was simply the pre-war parity; going back meant going back to 1914. The only problem was that wages now had to be forced down – not perhaps to their 1914 level but, say, 10 per cent below what was customary by the mid-1920s. This applied especially to British export industries, and even more to those export industries where wages comprised a large part of total costs. That meant coal. The long miners' strike of 1926, leading in the same year to Britain's only General Strike, was thus one of the economic consequences of going back on the Gold Standard at $4.86.

The Treasury model of the economy was based on the premise that all prices, including wages, were flexible. It followed that all internal prices could be expected to accommodate to a single external price, the exchange rate. For if prices were indeed flexible, the exact exchange rate set at any particular time did not really matter very much.

In theory Keynes accepted that an adjustment process could sort out any problems. His *Treatise* showed how it could be done – perhaps how it should be done. This was the general case; but he also outlined a special case, which was obviously applicable to Great Britain in 1930, when 'its international disequilibrium is involving it in severe unemployment'. Under those conditions, 'the Government must itself promote a programme of domestic investment'.[30] Everyone knew that he was the joint author of 'Can Lloyd George Do It?' As expected, therefore, he justified the same general approach to the Macmillan committee, and did so in a dialogue with the chairman at the end of February 1930.

'Does it come to this – that because we are not a closed nation the Bank rate cannot achieve the results?' Macmillan asked, showing the capacity of a good lawyer to pick up a new brief. 'There is also another reason,' Keynes replied. 'It could if we were a *fluid* system. For in that case, when we had a surplus of home investments over savings, the Bank rate could always force wages down to a level where exports would be adequate.' Macmillan took the point – 'It would be the principle of hydraulics.' 'Yes,' said Keynes; 'that is the beauty of the Bank rate.' To which Macmillan naturally responded with the key question: 'Why is it not fluid now?'[31]

It was a question that Keynes had been thinking about, in one form or another, for several years. It had certainly been on his mind since *The Economic Consequences of the Peace* (1919), and there are arguably some adumbrations in *Indian Currency and Finance* (1913). His objections to the reparations demanded of Germany arose essentially out of the impracticability of making such international transfers across the exchanges – an issue on which revisionist historians who take a more benign view of the Versailles Peace Treaty have yet to prove Keynes wrong.

The crude idea of making Germany 'pay' till the pips squeaked was flawed for more than moral or political reasons. It ignored the fact that it was not a heap of gold that would be transferred but rather a stream of goods that Germany would arbitrarily be required to export – or rather, provide free of charge. This would in fact require the German economy to become the mightiest in Europe, through an export miracle to be achieved despite the lack of any market incentive through payment! Such fantasies naturally ran up against the stubborn realities of the transfer problem. Keynes commented in 1928: 'Those who see no difficulty in this – like those who saw no difficulty in Great Britain's return to the Gold Standard – are applying the theory of liquids to what is, if not a solid, at least a sticky mass with strong internal resistance.'[32]

The authorities' ingrained assumptions about fluid or flexible prices account for much of their early hostility to Keynes's reasoning. They simply expected prices to behave as their model predicted. Thus in 1925 Niemeyer had dismissed Keynes's arguments in forthright terms – 'To me they seem sheer lunacy' – and had done so in the confidence that current economic trends were on his side.

He predicted that prices, and hence unemployment, would duly fall as the orthodox theories prescribed, in which case 'a good deal of Mr Keynes' argument will fade away'.[33]

Both of Niemeyer's predictions were wrong. Arguments about whether sterling was really overvalued in 1925 can actually be resolved by a simple test: whether the Bank of England needed to maintain a dear-money policy, year after year, in order to defend this parity. It did. This was naturally unpopular and, in Governor Norman's rueful phrase, meant that the bank was 'continuously under the harrow'.

In March 1930 Norman was finally ready to face his ordeal of examination by the Macmillan committee. Alas, he faced a committee already indoctrinated by Keynes. Worse still, Keynes himself would inevitably dominate the questioning. But even in the opening questions, led by Macmillan, the governor seemed unable to engage with the issues. His view that the 'actual ill-effects were greatly exaggerated and that they are more psychological than real' revealed some sense of distance from the coalfields. 'If a machine gets jammed it will not work,' Macmillan persisted, regurgitating his recent lessons from Keynes, but getting nowhere. Then Ernest Bevin, with his trade unionist experience, weighed in to make a link between wage reductions and the Gold Standard, but was repeatedly fobbed off by Norman. 'No, I do not think so.' 'I do not think as a necessary consequence.' 'No, I do not, Sir.'

Keynes took up the questioning. He naturally challenged Norman on his view that the workings of bank rate relied on psychology rather than hydraulics. Did this not repudiate orthodox theory? 'I did not mean to repudiate it, as I understand it,' said Norman. Keynes then gave him the benefit of a recapitulation of the orthodox theory, challenging Norman to indicate any dissent, but provoking only the response: 'I could not dispute it with you.' This hapless display finally provoked Professor Gregory to intervene. 'I thought we were trying to work out the theory of how the Bank rate is supposed to operate under present conditions,' he said impatiently, 'but if I am told that it does not work that way I am merely asking for an alternative explanation of how it does work.'[34] Nothing was forthcoming.

It was at this point that the authorities got seriously worried about the Macmillan committee. They had not liked the idea of open discussion of these mysteries in the first place. The private secretary to the Chancellor of the Exchequer had warned at the outset 'that we have had one continuous policy as a guiding principle and a system which is knave-proof', whereas 'the critics, especially Keynes, have changed their ideas and their theories nearly every year'. As a dutiful civil servant, he asked the minister: 'Is there not some danger of giving the impression that the Governor is being put in the dock?'[35] Norman's performance bore out such fears. One result was that the Treasury made sure that its own evidence was far, far better prepared, not least against Keynes's expected sniping at what was becoming known as the 'Treasury View'.

Keynes was simply having too much success in setting the agenda. But it would be wrong to suppose that he had hijacked the Macmillan committee, with a flight towards public works as the sudden new destination. For one thing, the other members were not ciphers and Keynes knew that he had to allow for a variety of opinions around the table. There were protectionist members. His ally McKenna favoured relaxation of monetary policy; his other ally, Bevin, thought devaluation might be better. In fact Keynes's private evidence had enumerated a range of possibilities for action – all of them accepting that wages were 'sticky' and that the deflationary adjustment process had therefore failed.

Keynes told the committee that there were seven possible remedies, given Britain's current predicament. One was indeed abandoning the parity of $4.86 – undoing the bad decision of 1925. But this could no longer be undone easily, since events had acquired their own momentum, and Keynes now regarded devaluation as a last resort. A second possibility was what later became known as incomes policy. This would involve a 'national treaty' to bring down all wages immediately to the required level, rather than leaving such adjustment to the slow and haphazard workings of the market. Keynes regarded this as equitable in theory but impracticable: a verdict that subsequent Keynesian experiments with incomes policies, especially in the 1960s and 1970s, in both Britain and the USA, have done little to qualify.

A third remedy was bounties to industry. This was functionally equivalent in so far as it meant subsidising wages in vulnerable industries, especially those most keenly subject to competition from overseas, thus spreading the pain across the whole community rather than letting one group of workers suffer. Like incomes policy, it had a political rather than an economic rationale, but unlike incomes policy was never subsequently to become serious politics. A fourth remedy – 'rationalisation' – was so vague that almost anybody, including Montagu Norman, could readily agree to it. It was a vogue word for schemes to cut unit costs, especially through economies of scale, and in so far as it meant greater efficiency it was a fine panacea. Everyone nodded, if only through weariness.

Next on Keynes's list came tariffs. Their possible relevance to a slump was timeless – what country has not heard the protectionist cry when facing hard times? 'British jobs for British workers' and 'Buy American' are the sort of slogans that have been around for a long time. Fears of exporting jobs to lower-paid workers overseas are not new. The belief that protectionist tariffs can increase home employment has often sounded plausible – except to economists. Moreover, in Britain tariffs were by far the most politically charged of Keynes's seven possible remedies, because Free Trade had become a sharp dividing line between the political parties for more than a quarter of a century. Thus Conservatives were generally sympathetic to tariffs, especially when they were given an imperial twist; while both Liberals and Labour had always been entrenched upholders of Free Trade. For Keynes even to broach the idea was not only shocking but also evidence of his genuine open-mindedness.

His reasoning becomes apparent in relation to his sixth policy option. This was, of course, home investment or public works. Keynes came clean in calling it 'my favourite remedy – the one to which I attach much the greatest importance'. It was the option available to a country under the special case of the *Treatise*, when a jam or hitch in the workings of the Gold Standard mechanism thwarted the achievement of equilibrium by the natural process of market adjustments. But actually it was simpler than that: 'It always seems to me that this argument is quite agreeable to common sense.' Moreover, as Keynes put it, 'I think the first impetus forward must come from action of this kind, that it must be Government investment which will break the vicious circle.'[36]

As he had since 1924, he presented a line of argument that we can fairly identify as Keynesian. But in 1930, it should be noted, the argument took the Gold Standard as a given, thus justifying resort to public works – and much the same reasoning justified tariffs too, as another special case, only valid under such conditions. Both, then, were presented as second-best options, given both a fixed exchange rate and the inflexibility of prices.

Finally, Keynes proposed international measures as his seventh remedy for the Macmillan committee. Since high interest rates were the problem, and since they were high because of international pressure, the obvious solution was international agreement by all countries simultaneously to bring down interest rates. Like Free Trade, this seemed a simple means of increasing the wealth of nations to the benefit of all – simple but not easy. In the 1930s Keynes largely despaired of gaining agreement from enough countries to make this sort of remedy feasible. Instead of wasting time in chasing the unattainable, he encouraged each country, and especially Britain and the United States, to seek its own salvation through expansionist measures, whether or not protectionist. Only in the 1940s, as we have seen, was he to play a key role in creating a sort of international Keynesianism, with institutions that accepted full employment alongside free trade as goals.

'What I am trying to do is to do justice to all the remedies that have been put forward,' Keynes told the committee. 'I think I said at the beginning that there was something to be said for all of them.'[37] By and large, this is what he did: making the best case in good faith for the relevance of each, while not concealing his own preference. This was consistent with his long-standing view that every option deserved to be considered. It was consistent too with his quest for second-best options, under changing conditions, rather than a doctrinaire attachment to the ideal. And it was, of course, a gift to his critics who, now as then, have always delighted in discrediting Keynes on the grounds of his alleged inconsistency.

Paralleling Keynes's membership of the Macmillan committee, he was also appointed in 1930 as a member of the government's new Economic Advisory Council (EAC). In this forum, too, much the same diverse policy options were canvassed, by Keynes as by other EAC members. And it was in this capacity that Keynes explained to the Prime Minister, Ramsay MacDonald, that 'the peculiarity of my position lies, perhaps, in the fact that I am in favour of practically all the remedies which have been suggested in any quarter. Some of them are better than others. But nearly all of them seem to tend in the right direction.' The conclusion he drew was consistent in its scorn for 'long-run' strategies of inertia: 'The unforgivable attitude is, therefore, for me the negative one, – the repelling of each of these remedies in turn.'[38]

It is easy to understand why Keynes had clashed with Treasury orthodoxy in the late 1920s. 'To all well-laid schemes of progress and enterprise, they have (whenever they could) barred the door with, No!', so 'Can Lloyd George Do It?' claimed. In this avowedly political pamphlet, the Conservative philosophy was contemptuously caricatured: 'You must not try to employ everyone, because this will cause inflation. You must not invest, because how can you know that it will pay? You must not do anything, because this will only mean that you can't do something else.'[39]

This identified a mindset rather than a particular argument as the obstacle. 'But we are not tottering to our graves,' ran the peroration. 'We are healthy children. We need the breath of life. There is nothing to be afraid of. On the contrary. The future holds in store for us far more wealth and economic freedom and possibilities of personal life than the past has ever offered.'[40] Nobody has a copyright on the rhetoric of hope and audacity and those who detected a Keynesian note in President Obama's inaugural address in January 2009 have a point.

Conservative rhetoric, by contrast, had found no finer exponent than Winston Churchill. His statement on Budget day in 1929 had endorsed 'the orthodox Treasury dogma, which is steadfastly held, that whatever might be the political or social advantages, very little additional employment and no permanent additional employment can in fact, and as a general rule, be created by State borrowing and State expenditure'.[41] With his knack for spotting the telling quotation, Keynes had seized on Churchill's words, the better to expose this dogma as fallacious. The 'Treasury View' quickly became a term of art, in much its modern sense (or perhaps a sense that can be traced back to the early-nineteenth-century economist David Ricardo). It is the proposition that any increase in government spending on public works will 'crowd out' an equivalent amount of private investment, and thus fail to reduce overall unemployment.

The Treasury knew in advance that Keynes would attack its eponymous dogma. The urbane figure of Sir Frederick Leith-

Ross could be seen at virtually every meeting of the Macmillan committee in early 1930, spying out the ground for his colleagues in the Treasury. He thus heard Keynes's opinion of 'the so-called "Treasury View"' in March – 'that it is a pure logical delusion, without any foundation at all in sound thinking'. Keynes said that this was because the proposition failed to distinguish between savings and investment, in the way that his own analysis did in the *Treatise*. But he did not demand the adoption of his own peculiar terminology to sustain his central point: 'The Treasury view only demonstrates that home investment is not a cure for unemployment, by first of all assuming – in effect – that there is no unemployment to cure.' At full employment, crowding-out may indeed be an inflationary hazard; but only then. So he called the Treasury View 'the natural result of standing half-way between common sense and sound theory; it is the result of having abandoned the one without having reached the other'.[42]

The Treasury knew better than to debate at this level. 'The fact is that Keynes, like other economists, lives in a world of abstractions,' the clubbable 'Leithers' reported back to his colleagues. 'He speaks of "Industry", "Profits", "Losses", "Price level" as if they were realities.'[43] There is a good point here, of course. How far can any proposition in economic theory be applied to the intractable difficulties of a world where everything turns out to be much more complex and muddled than under the conditions airily specified, for the sake of simplicity, in economic theory?

When Keynes asked why an impoverished country could not solve its problems by simultaneously mobilising unused savings and unemployed workers, the rhetorical appeal was beguiling. Yet the Treasury surely had a point too. It was only doing its job in advising ministers that these eloquent pleas should be tempered with some necessary caution; that it is necessary not to alarm public opinion, especially about the scale of expenditure; that ministers should investigate any public works proposal for what we would call its 'shovel-ready' status; and that any hopes of easy success should be tempered by the Treasury's own hard-won experience (which ministers should be aware has often been frankly rather disappointing).

Leith-Ross, a man of the world, was shrewd enough to spot the weak points in the authorities' case. 'Mr J. M. Keynes says that, despite the general reduction of price levels since 1925, there has been no appreciable reduction during the same period in the rates of wages paid to labour in the United Kingdom,' he wrote, with evident puzzlement, to his Treasury colleague R. G. Hawtrey, an old friend of Keynes. Leith-Ross expostulated to Hawtrey, who was paid to know things like this, that 'it appears to be so surprising that I should be glad if you would go into it'.[44] Hawtrey duly turned up the relevant indexes, checked the figures: alas, it was so, and Keynes was right in what he had told the Macmillan committee. Not until March 1930, therefore, did the Treasury wake up to the news that British prices and wages were disobeying the laws of economic theory about their axiomatic flexibility.

So neither in theory nor in practice did the authorities have as good a hand to play as they had once supposed. The Treasury View was altogether too tendentious; and the brute facts seemed to vindicate Keynes rather than the Treasury, still less the Bank of England, in the argument about prices, wages and unemployment. This being so, it was clearly politic to adopt a less trenchant tone in the Treasury evidence. Luckily the post of controller of finance and supply services at the Treasury was no longer occupied by the abrasive, doctrinaire Niemeyer but by the emollient, pragmatic Sir Richard Hopkins. When he went in May 1930 to meet the committee, over whom Keynes had established an alarming intellectual ascendancy, it was Hopkins's moment.

The Treasury team were working well together. Well-briefed by 'Leithers', and well-prepared himself, 'Hoppy' executed an adroit tactical retreat from an exposed position. Instead, his brief was to plead not only administrative feasibility but confidence as the real problems – 'so far from setting up a cycle of prosperity' or inducing 'a general willingness to invest in these vast Government loans I should have thought that the loans would have to be put out at a very high price, and that the process might be accompanied by despondency on the part of general business, rather than otherwise'.[45] Hopkins's forte was his non-adversarial tone, his refusal to rise to gladiatorial display. 'I would like time to think it over' and 'I should like time to consider this' constituted his line in repartee. 'I am a layman with regard to control of the Bank Rate and control of the currency,' he pleaded on the first day of his evidence, avoiding the pitfalls that had ensnared Norman two months earlier.[46]

On the second and final day of his evidence, Hopkins finally faced Keynes's questioning. They were well matched. 'I think the Treasury view has sometimes been rather compendiously and not very accurately stated,' Hopkins began, helped from the chair by Macmillan, who queried whether it had been 'a little misunderstood?' Yes, Hopkins readily agreed, 'a little misunderstood'. Disowning dogma, Hopkins dwelt instead on two much more durable objections to any proposals for public works: not only whether they are shovel-ready but also whether they will command public confidence. 'It seems to me,' mused Hopkins, 'that a feeling might widely arise that this was a project of extravagance and waste.'[47] The fact is that exactly such a feeling was entertained by his own colleagues. We can literally see this because the official Treasury copy of the Liberal pamphlet 'We Can Conquer Unemployment', preserved in the National Archives, has been defaced. To Lloyd George's message, 'We Mobilised for War, Let us Mobilise for Prosperity', three words have been added by the Treasury wits – 'EXTRAVAGANCE, INFLATION, BANKRUPTCY'.

Nothing so gross escaped Hopkins's lips in his evidence. He put the problem at one remove, by pointing to the effect of such negative sentiments, whether or not warranted, in undermining confidence. 'If Mr Bevin could assure you that the schemes would be popular, then you would say that they would cure unemployment?' asked Keynes. 'No,' parried Hopkins. 'You are asking me to say that if I

The official copy of the Liberal pamphlet in the National Archives shows the real Treasury View in opposing Keynesian proposals in 1929–30.

thought that the public sentiment would endorse the large plan to which we are referring, then it would cure our situation.' Keynes pounced: 'Yes?' Hopkins was not allowing everything to turn on this – 'But I went on to say that there were other difficulties.'

Keynes knew that he had to face these detailed, practical objections. But he also expected to meet the 'crowding-out' proposition and make this the decisive argument. Yet here the Treasury now appeared virtually Viewless. 'It bends so much that I find difficulty in getting hold of it?' Keynes asked. 'Yes,' Hopkins blandly agreed; 'I do not think these views are capable of being put in the form of a theoretical doctrine.'[48]

'I think we may characterise it as a drawn battle!' said the chairman at the end.[49] It still seems a fair verdict; and Harrod thought that, in resisting Keynes on his own ground, Hopkins had 'a unique distinction in his generation'.[50] But the point was, of course, that Hopkins had shifted the ground, focusing on points where his own expertise outmatched that of Keynes, and raising queries that still demand answers today when infrastructure proposals are put forward.

One telling indication of the cogency of Hopkins's points is that he had by now privately convinced Keynes's former collaborator, Hubert Henderson. Recently appointed to a Civil Service post as secretary of the EAC, by 1930 Henderson was busily backtracking from what 'Can Lloyd George Do It?' had argued in 1929. 'My first shifting of opinion from my position a year or so ago, is that I am less disposed to regard (I don't say our 2 million unemployment) but our 1,200,000 unemployment as a short-period transitional problem, yielding to the treatment of a purely temporary stimulus,' he told Keynes in a letter. So the cost to the budget could not be airily dismissed and nor could the psychology of the business community. 'It won't therefore be a case of their *saying* they're alarmed: they *will* be alarmed,' said Henderson, and accused Keynes of making light of such difficulties because he was 'over-moved by a sense that it's inconsistent with your self-respect to accept anything savouring of a conservative conclusion'.[51]

Henderson knew Keynes well. They had been academic colleagues, political allies, literary collaborators. On Keynes's own psychology, Henderson was not wholly wrong. The breach between them was temperamental as much as anything else, and their own mutual confidence did not really survive Henderson's final taunt (quoted more fully above in the Introduction) that Keynes might end up as 'the man who persuaded the British people to ruin themselves by gambling on a greater illusion than any of those which he had shattered'. Henderson's defection shows that the arguments of 1929, directed at a British unemployment total of around 10 per cent, were being overtaken by events, as the official figures reached 15 per cent in May 1930 and pushed over 20 per cent at the end of that year.

Henderson responded by becoming more conservative in his analysis: Keynes by becoming more radical. Both, in their different ways, became more aware of the importance of confidence, which is one reason why both were ready to accept tariffs, if only because the ordinary Conservative businessman would be favourably impressed.

The Treasury's tame economist, Ralph Hawtrey, had been allowed to give his own evidence to the Macmillan committee. Hawtrey was a strong upholder of a monetary analysis of the causes of the problem; but so, at that time, was Keynes. Where they differed was that Hawtrey also believed that the solution should come through monetary policy. He did not believe in public works but in the expansion of credit that would be necessary to finance them – what others saw as the inflationary danger. Hawtrey was to state in 1932 that 'people who regard the word inflation as necessarily having a bad sense would call this degree of expansion "reflation" '.[52] He was thus one of the first British economists to import this term from Hoover's America. It is useful in making the point that reflation may be exactly what we need when the danger we face is that of deflation.

Hawtrey, then, for all his official employment, was no supporter of Norman's orthodoxy at the Bank of England. Norman defended the gold reserves at all costs. Hawtrey, by contrast, believed that 'it would have been worth getting rid of £100,000,000 of gold to cure unemployment' by lowering interest rates. Explaining his own reflationary credit policy, Hawtrey told the committee that 'the way to conjure outlay out of the fourth dimension is to lower the Bank Rate'. Hearing him, the banker McKenna demanded clarification: 'Your whole argument is turned upon cheap money?' 'Yes,' Hawtrey readily agreed.[53] This was a repudiation of Bank of England policy and it showed Hawtrey more ready to take risks with the reserves than was Keynes.

Like Keynes, however, Hawtrey relied on the theoretical proposition that it was interest rate that brought saving and investment into equilibrium. Indeed an assumption of this sort was common to almost all economists at the time. What divided them was the practical issue of what to do when faced with any kind of obstruction, jam, hitch, rigidity or stickiness in the actual workings of the system.

This is apparent from Professor A. C. Pigou's appearance before the committee at the end of May 1930. He was much more cautious in expression than Keynes, more reserved, more qualified, more ambivalent; but essentially in agreement on pragmatic, second-best policy options. Since there was 'an obstruction to the free working of economic forces', it followed that 'forms of State interference which, if there were no obstruction, would do harm, will in fact do good'. As he affirmed: 'This is a very important principle.' This was why, in an emergency, he favoured 'devices' or 'gadgets', including 'large Government expenditure on really useful public works'.[54] As he wrote in a letter to *The Times* a week later, advocating public works, the Treasury View was a good reason against state action 'provided that there were no unemployment to reduce!'[55] Keynes could hardly have expected better support from 'the Prof.'.

Pigou's evidence explicitly informed his advice to the EAC. He was a member of the small committee of economists that it had set up under Keynes's chairmanship, as was their former Cambridge colleague turned civil servant, Hubert Henderson. Sir Josiah Stamp, who had a longer experience of advising government than any other British economist, was a member: an affable, capable man of affairs who got on well with Keynes. The final member was Lionel Robbins, who was later to work so closely with Keynes in wartime, and was currently a very new professor at the LSE, not yet thirty-two and not yet even listed in *Who's Who*.

Yet it was Robbins, with the courage of his youthful doctrinaire convictions, who found himself isolated. He resisted all Keynes's wiles in trying to get an agreed report, countenancing both public works and tariffs. The others pragmatically, often regretfully, acquiesced in trying both these remedies, given the wicked world they lived in. Robbins alone bravely dissented. And it was not so much the endorsement of public works as the surrender to tariffs that proved non-negotiable. 'Some economists in this country, despairing of the rigidity of money wages, may have turned to Protection as a desperate expedient,' Robbins wrote, fairly accurately summing up his colleagues' decision to sully the Free Trade principles on which they had all been brought up.[56] It was thus Robbins who stuck to principle while the leaders of his profession, despite sharing much the same orthodox principles, can be called pragmatic Marshallians – Keynes among them.

Whether Lloyd George could have 'done it' in 1929–30 has long been debated. In fact, the Labour Government, while not going as far as the proposals in 'Can Lloyd George Do It?', approved substantial public works schemes, though, as Hopkins well knew, many proved not to be shovel-ready. The best modern estimates of the effect of a public works programme of £100 million, given the fixed exchange rate under the Gold Standard, show a range between about 350,000 and 480,000 extra jobs created.[57] This is lower than the estimate in 'Can Lloyd George Do It?', of 500,000 new jobs; and by 1930 unemployment itself had risen. But the stimulus is not all that far short of what reasonably appeared to be needed in 1929, when the pledge was given, to reduce the million unemployed of 1929 to 'normal' proportions. The final irony is that the variations in these estimates depend crucially on what value is specified for the 'multiplier' – a concept that had yet to revolutionise Keynesian economics.

The Macmillan Report was published in July 1931. It was a largely consensual document, more productive in analysis than in action. There was an addendum, urging an active policy including both public works and tariffs, signed by six out of fourteen members, led by the triumvirate of Keynes, Bevin and McKenna. Devaluation was also mentioned in hushed tones. Almost immediately, the report was swamped by the tsunami of the financial and political crisis. By August the Labour Government had collapsed. By September Britain was off the Gold Standard. By October the National Government had won a landslide electoral victory; and Neville Chamberlain, now Chancellor of the Exchequer, had his own ideas about tariffs (positive) and public works (negative).

So the report had little immediate impact on policy. The Macmillan committee's exhaustive discussions, however, provided not only a unique record of Keynes in action, urging an economic stimulus: they also provided a stimulus of an intellectual kind that was to affect his thinking in fundamental ways.

4

'Animal spirits'
Rethinking economic theory

Looking backward, we know Keynes as the man who wrote the *General Theory*. But Keynes himself, living his life forward, naturally thought, while in the throes of composition, that the *Treatise* would be his *magnum opus*. During the first nine months of 1930, he was occupied in an overlapping way with the sittings of the Macmillan committee, then with the meetings of the EAC's committee of economists, and all along with the final revisions of the *Treatise* for publication in October. As we have seen, there was much interplay between these different discussions of economic policy – and of theory too.

Keynes wanted his analysis in the *Treatise* to inform current debates about practical policy. 'We quite realise we are getting the fruits of your research presented to us in a form in which we can understand it,' Lord Macmillan had said in February. Keynes responded that his work had 'been read now by some of the principal economists of Cambridge, who did not all start sympathetic to it, but they are now satisfied, I think, that it is accurate'.[1] He was referring in particular to his colleague Dennis Robertson (ultimately Pigou's successor in the chair of Political Economy at Cambridge); and also to Ralph Hawtrey, who saw the proofs of the *Treatise* before he gave his own evidence to the committee and who continued to write lengthy private criticisms, draft after draft, nailing down Keynes's inconsistencies.

The *Treatise* was due to be published before the Macmillan committee was due to report. 'Therefore it will be exposed to the hostile criticism of the world for an appreciable time,' Keynes assured Macmillan.[2] Meanwhile Keynes himself had no doubts about the soundness of its analysis: that if total investment was less than total savings then losses and unemployment must be the result. 'This, of course, is a difficult theoretical proposition,' he told Governor Norman in May 1930. 'It is very important that a competent decision should be reached whether it is true or false. I can only say that I am ready to have my head chopped off if it is false!'[3]

Some of these confident expectations, however, did not survive for long. In September, with publication now imminent, Maynard told Florence Keynes that his seven years of work on the *Treatise* was now done, but with some dissatisfaction now intermingled with his relief: 'Artistically it is a failure – I have changed my mind too much during the course of it for it to be a proper unity.'[4]

Try as he might, he could not kick this terrible habit of his. The great economist Friedrich von Hayek was currently a colleague of Gregory and Robbins at the LSE, the citadel of economic orthodoxy. Hayek devoted a two-part article for the LSE house journal *Economica* to a critique of Keynes's big book, only to find that, after the second instalment of this long review appeared in February 1932, 'he told me that he had in the meantime changed his mind and no longer believed what he had said in that work'.[5] Likewise, while Hawtrey continued dutifully poring over the *Treatise*, its author, far from digging in to defend it, was speaking by May 1932 of 'working it out all over again'.[6]

Whatever had happened to produce such an extraordinary retreat? Or was it perhaps an advance, this time in a more promising direction?

The criticisms of Robertson and Hawtrey had eventually sunk in. They were listened to precisely because each was so close to Keynes: personally as well as intellectually. They were seen as accomplices in his daredevil escape from a prison that Keynes subsequently labelled 'classical economics'. Since he meant by this 'a compact and coherent pre-war theory of economics to which most senior economists still subscribe', most of the profession were inmates. Orthodox economics assumed that the system reached its own equilibrium through the effect of interest rates in reconciling the level of investment to the amount of saving available – through flexible prices, of course. 'Before the war we were all classical economists,' Keynes asserted. 'I taught it myself to Robertson, undoubting and unrebuked.'[7]

Robertson had for years been Keynes's closest collaborator. Like a couple in the terminal stages of a marriage, they spent years and years arguing about money (in their case, the theory of money and credit and banking and prices). The apparatus of the *Treatise* thus owed a lot to Robertson, since he too believed that there was no reason to assume that saving and investment must harmonise. Robertson too thought that there might well be a mismatch, with investment deficient, savings excessive. And Robertson too thought that the Treasury View was therefore nonsense since public works could turn unused savings into valuable capital assets.

Robertson was no monetarist. He did not think (as Hawtrey did) that it was simply the expansion of credit, or monetary policy, that would prove effective. Robertson did not accept that cheap money alone could do the trick in the midst of a depression. When he had appeared before the Macmillan committee, he had been pressed by Keynes on this point, arguing that surely entrepreneurs would borrow more when interest rates fell low enough. 'But I still think there is a difficulty of the lenders coming forward,' Robertson responded – pointing to a paralysing lack of confidence when even an interest rate of 1 per cent might fail to stimulate investment.[8]

We can well recognise such a situation today, with the dramatic drop in interest rates in 2008–9. We are all aware of how, none the less, investors can remain risk-averse, while lenders become anxious not to tie up their money. A modern economist will probably want to shout 'liquidity preference' at this point. For, since the *General Theory*, the idea has become familiar that, when a slump has undermined confidence, low interest rates may not in themselves be enough to revive investment. People may simply prefer the liquidity of holding their wealth in money rather than accepting what they see as the miserably low – but to them appallingly risky – returns on the available investments. It is an insight that is as relevant today as eighty years ago.

It was Robertson, however, not Keynes who glimpsed this possibility in 1930, as they later reminded each other. The paradox is that, not only did Robertson abstain from writing his own revolutionary theoretical work: he could not, in the end, even accept the message of his friend's *General Theory* in 1936. The breach between them was really psychological as much as economic. Keynes told Robertson at this point that 'in truth, you are the only writer where much of it is to be found in embryo and to whom acknowledgements are due', and he perceptively added: 'So unlike me! I, perhaps, am too ready to take pleasure in feeling that my mind is changed; you too ready to take pain.'[9]

Hence it was Keynes who picked up the ball and ran with it. In the *Treatise*, to be sure, he had written about the 'bearishness' of the public. But in subsequently debating this with Robertson, Keynes went further. He needed to dispel the widely held impression that, when he talked about saving exceeding investment, he meant that 'hoarding' produced tangible 'idle savings', sitting in bank accounts or elsewhere. This was not Keynes's view (though Hayek thought it was). So Keynes sought to clarify his meaning by explaining that 'hoarding' was not an actual *process* but a psychological *motive*. And instead of talking about 'bearishness' to explain the public's reluctance to make investments, he started talking about the 'propensity to hoard' instead.[10] Under fire, he was refashioning his conceptual tools. As early as the end of 1931, Keynes told a graduate student in Hayek's department at the LSE (Nicholas Kaldor, later himself a professor at Cambridge): 'I must be more lucid next time', and explained that he was now 'endeavouring to express the whole thing over again more clearly and from a different angle'.[11]

A lot of trouble stems from the way that the *Treatise* defines saving and investment. Rhetorically, it suits Keynes nicely to maintain that they need not be equal. It is the implicit assumption that they are bound to be equal, achieving equilibrium automatically and painlessly, that he wants to expose. In this respect, the vision is the same in the *Treatise* or the *General Theory*, for in Keynes's view, it is investment that is active, saving passive in this relationship. He wants to show how the dynamics of the economy depend on the extent to which enterprise is or is not rewarded (in building cities, draining fens, etc.). If expectations are cheated in outcome, entrepreneurs make losses. Thrift is thus in the dock, not enterprise.

Then the *Treatise* takes a false step. It makes the dramatic but vulnerable claim that the losses are equal to the excess of saving over investment. The problem is that the rhetorical effect needs to be squared with mathematical logic. Here the *Treatise* has to make its 'fundamental equations' add up by using a peculiar definition. Income is defined as *expected* income, including expected profit, but excluding 'windfall' gains or losses. If expectations are fulfilled, savings are indeed equal to investment. Both have essentially the same definition: the residual part of income that is not consumed.

How, then, can savings and investment be different? Because, even if the expected profit fails to materialise, the *Treatise* still counts it as part of 'income'. And since this notionally inflated 'income' minus actual consumption equals savings, it follows that 'savings' too must be notionally inflated by exactly the same amount. Income is obviously different from actual receipts because it includes this fairy gold – profits that entrepreneurs initially expected to make but fail to receive in a falling market. So it is indeed the case that business losses (the shortfall between expected 'income' and actual receipts) must be the same as the excess of 'savings' (the part of 'income' that is neither consumed nor profitably invested). But neither this slice of 'income' nor these 'excess savings' actually materialise. Both are really measures of unfulfilled expectations.

Robertson and Hawtrey, each in his own way, tried to get this across to Keynes. Hawtrey summed up by saying that of course the *Treatise* was correct in claiming that the excess of savings over investment equalled business losses, precisely because 'the excess savings *are* the losses made by the entrepreneurs and have no other existence whatever'.[12] So what Keynes had spent so much energy in maintaining was not so much a truth as a truism. Both he and Hawtrey, it should be remembered, had studied mathematics as undergraduates. As Keynes told his students in one of his lectures at Cambridge: 'The whole of mathematics is a truism and truisms help to clear one's mind.'[13]

His own mind became considerably clearer by 1932. We can now see that he was moving beyond a monetary understanding of the way the economy works, assuming that all adjustments depend essentially on changes in prices. 'Classical' economics – really Marshallian orthodoxy – said that an infinitely adjustable price mechanism will deliver equilibrium via interest rates.

Suppose, however, that such adjustments work not through changes in prices, but changes in total output itself. Keynes had previously suggested such possibilities in the real world, when prices are sticky, but in theory he had always insisted that sufficiently low interest rates will do the trick. It was actually

Hawtrey who was more alive to the possibility that the level of output itself might respond first. Indeed Hawtrey sketched a model of the economy in which deflation and inflation (or reflation) result in cumulative changes in the level of total income and output; but neither he nor Keynes saw the full significance of where this might lead (though, again, a modern economist might mutter about a multiplier effect).

A lot of these discussions would have been simpler, as Keynes later admitted, if he had known earlier of an idea introduced by the Swedish economist Gunnar Myrdal and developed by his compatriot Bertil Ohlin. This was the simple but compelling distinction between *ex ante* (how things are intended) and *ex post* (how they actually work out). Of course Keynes could have used this decades earlier in his academic work, to explain that his theory of probability rested on *ex ante* judgements, made in advance, not on *ex post* outcomes.

We are surely entitled to anticipate his own awareness of this distinction in the interests of clarity. For what Keynes was more clumsily saying in March 1932, when he conceded the argument over the definition of 'savings' and 'income' to Robertson, Hawtrey and Hayek, turned on exactly this point. Yes, he admitted, in adopting the conventional definition, 'the sense to which I have now bowed the knee': the *Treatise* had talked about both saving and income *ex ante*, from the viewpoint of expectations.

The key point, to which Keynes adhered, was that the expectations had not been realised. So he now accepted the *ex post* definitions, which could be called simple-minded or common sense. Savings were thus actual realised savings and always equal in the end to the prior investment. But Keynes warned that 'the implications of this use of language are decidedly different from what "common-sense" supposes' – because, *ex post*, saving 'always and necessarily accommodates itself' to investment, passively. Thrift does not determine enterprise. Instead, enterprise actively determines thrift, through a change in the total level of income. In fact, saving is 'no longer the dog, which common sense believes it to be, but the tail'.[14]

Here was the seed of the Keynesian revolution in economic theory. It was not yet a flower. But the ground had been cleared for the seed to take root. We can now see why Keynes later said that 'in recent times, I have never regarded Hawtrey, Robertson or Ohlin, for example, as classical economists'.[15] He meant it as a tribute when he wrote for publication in 1937: 'I regard Mr Hawtrey as my grandparent and Mr Robertson as my parent in the paths of errancy, and I have been greatly influenced by them.'[16] This is consistent with what Keynes told Robertson in a private letter. 'The last thing I should accuse you of is being classical or orthodox,' he wrote. 'But you won't slough your skins, like a good snake!'[17]

There was another reason for Keynes to slough off an old skin. This was the influence of his younger colleagues in Cambridge. At the beginning of 1931, their small discussion circle, or 'Circus', began meeting regularly to discuss the recently published *Treatise*. The core members were Austin Robinson, soon to be assistant editor of the *Economic Journal* and much later to be promoted to a chair in the Economics Faculty; his left-wing wife Joan Robinson, who had the singular distinction of ultimately succeeding her husband in the same chair; Piero Sraffa, subsequently famous for his edition of the works of the classical economist David Ricardo; Richard Kahn, a twenty-five-year-old Fellow of King's College for whom Keynes had secured temporary employment in 1930 as joint secretary of the EAC's committee of economists; and James Meade, the future Nobel laureate, then a novice economist of twenty-three, in Cambridge just for one academic year to learn his trade before taking up a teaching Fellowship in Oxford.

The Circus thrashed out their problems between themselves, usually reporting back to the busy, famous, peripatetic Keynes through Kahn, whom he knew best. Schumpeter was aware of the Circus, impressed that he himself had nothing like it, and later suggested that its members, especially Kahn, had been given insufficient credit. This was a Harvard view, already more professionally sharp than 1930s Cambridge. The fact is that the Circus and Keynes alike had a deplorably weak sense of individual intellectual property by the standards of the modern research culture. They all borrowed from each other without generating feelings that anyone had been robbed, still less talking of plagiarism. As Austin Robinson later put it, Keynes 'had a wonderful memory for arguments, but no memory for their authors'.[18]

Meade's position was at once marginal and pivotal. He was the new boy; he only stayed in Cambridge for a year; he had to return to his post in Oxford before October 1931; yet he firmly believed that he then took with him the essentials of the theory of effective demand. This claim, moreover, withstands scrutiny because of what he contributed to one of the most famous conceptual breakthroughs in the history of economics.

This was the 'multiplier' concept, as Keynes called it after he had later appropriated it. It had its origin in a short paper that Kahn had prepared for the EAC's committee of economists in 1930. This was an exercise addressed to two awkward questions, still obviously relevant today, about any public works proposal. First, how much new employment can it actually be expected to generate? Secondly, how to pay for it?

Kahn focused on the first question. It had been tackled in 1929 in 'Can Lloyd George Do It?', with the argument that, as well as the workers actually employed on new roads, indirect employment would provide a further boost. 'The fact that many workpeople who are now unemployed would be receiving wages instead of unemployment pay would mean an increase in effective purchasing power which would give a general stimulus to trade.'[19] This sounds like common sense and it is not wrong. But it might prompt a vague notion that this sort of cumulative prosperity can be infinite in its repercussions. That sounds – and is – too good to be true.

Kahn's achievement was to show that the effects are finite and that they can be specified. The process itself might have an infinite number of repercussions, but these will always sum to a finite figure, which can be calculated. The key is what *proportion* of extra new income in the hands of a newly employed worker will be passed on in the form of spending – the more the better for multiplying the stimulative effect.

If, say, half is spent, then this expenditure in turn is subject to the same arithmetic – half of half (or a quarter) will be spent, and then half of that (an eighth), and so on. The final arithmetic here, dividing by 2 each time along the infinitely long chain of spending, will in aggregate *multiply* the original investment by 2, meaning that, in this case, it will have twice the leverage of the initial stimulus package.

Kahn's was a great achievement. Every subsequent attempt to specify the effects of a stimulus package in a determinate way rests on this model. If half is spent, the multiplier is 2, which is simple and elegant for demonstration purposes. It is also, in fact, the sort of thing that early enthusiasts for the multiplier excitedly told each other, including Keynes, who based his own later calculations on a multiplier of 2, and expected the multiplier to be, if anything, higher than that in the United States in the 1930s. Actually, modern estimates of the multiplier are lower, generally in the range 1.25 to 1.75. The *principle* of the multiplier, however, is the real discovery. For this analytical tool is as indispensable for those who use low estimates to argue against stimulus as it is for those who argue in favour.

In 1930, when first offered to the EAC's committee of economists in a primitive form, however, the tool was spurned. It needed to be sharpened and refashioned before its utility was acknowledged.

This is where the reflective, analytical mind of Meade came into play. As a result of the Circus discussions, Kahn incorporated a new idea into his famous 'multiplier' article, as published in mid-1931 in the *Economic Journal*, under Keynes's editorship. This further concept was called 'Mr Meade's Relation' – a usage which had been common among the members of the Circus (though when Keynes attended one of their meetings and heard of it for the first time, he apparently looked around the room for this unfamiliar member of Meade's family).

Mr Meade's Relation tells us to add up, at each stage, the amount that is *not* passed on in increased consumption. This is essentially a *generalisation* of the multiplier relationship, so that it follows each alternative process, either of spending or non-spending (saving). Kahn was focused on the extra employment generated by increments of spending; Meade was also looking at the extent to which either prices or output will rise in response to an initial investment – through increments of saving.

What are these 'leakages', as Keynes was later to call them? Personal savings seem to us the most obvious (though overlooked initially by Meade). 'Savings on the dole' had often been mentioned, meaning the relief to government and any other finances that had previously supported unemployed workers now back at work and supporting themselves. To this Meade adds increased import costs, since this is a leakage out of the pipeline of repercussive spending at home. And he adds any increase in unspent profits – real profits this time, constituting real savings put aside out of the new prosperity. These are all parts of the original investment that are not passed on in spending – and must therefore, by subtraction, be classed as saving. (This only seems odd if we forget that saving is passive, as distinct from investment, which is actually a form of spending on capital goods.) So income minus consumption equals saving, in the common-sense terms to which Keynes 'bent the knee' after abandoning *Treatise* definitions.

Meade's conclusion is another mind-clearing truism. For these unspent fractions of non-spending, in their parallel long series, *inexorably sum to unity*. Mr Meade's Relation thus indicates a source of saving that must exactly equal the original investment.

This highly significant conclusion can be put in two ways. One is to point out, as he and Kahn did at the time, that this gave the answer to the question: how to pay for public works? The answer is still valid: that, in the end, they pay for themselves out of the increased economic activity that they stimulate. The savings that are eventually generated are passive, and therefore permissive in providing sources that allow (but do not require) active investment to be accomplished.

The only *decision* involved is to make the investment in the first place. Public works indeed normally require borrowing the funds that will initially finance them – pump-priming is one analogy (though not a term used by Kahn or Meade or Keynes). The borrowing, admittedly, creates a debt to be settled in the future. But the allegation that this creates a burden of debt upon the next generation ignores the fact that they will simultaneously be made more prosperous by exactly the process that the borrowing initially financed.

Another way of expressing Meade's point is even more fundamental. For if this is true of an increment of investment for public works, it is surely true of all investment. What Mr Meade's Relation demonstrates is that saving will always be brought into equality with investment via a change in the level of total output or income. This is, in fact, the general process that brings an equilibrium between saving and investment. Little wonder that, forty years later, Meade wrote (in an echo of words that Keynes had used himself): 'Keynes's intellectual revolution was to shift economists from thinking normally in terms of a model of reality in which a dog called *savings* wagged his tail labelled *investment* to thinking in term of a model in which a dog called *investment* wagged his tail labelled *savings*.'[20]

It is not altogether clear how quickly the new thinking of the Circus was appreciated by Keynes at the time. Joan Robinson inimitably thought that he was very slow to catch on and that 'there were moments when we had some trouble in getting Maynard to see what the point of his revolution really was'.[21] In the summer of 1931, admittedly, Keynes was still giving public lectures in Chicago denying that saving and investment were necessarily equal, so he plainly had not yet jettisoned the *Treatise* definitions altogether. Yet some of the book's examples, almost despite its formal analysis, were leading the Circus into new paths.

Take the banana parable. This had first been produced by Keynes for the Macmillan committee. 'Let us suppose a community which owns nothing but banana plantations which they labour to cultivate,' he began. They produce bananas, they consume bananas, and nothing else. What they do not spend on bananas, they save; and the investment in the production of bananas exactly equals this saving. 'Into this Eden,' Keynes continued, 'there enters a thrift campaign urging the members of the public to abate their improvident practice of spending nearly all their current incomes on buying bananas for food.' For whatever reason, increased saving is not matched by increased investment – why should it be? Bananas are then produced in the same quantities as before; they will not keep; they have to be sold; but thrift has reduced the amount the public will pay for them; so the bananas are sold at lower prices.

'The only effect has been to transfer the wealth of the entrepreneurs out of their pockets into the pockets of the public,' claimed Keynes, always the champion of enterprise rather than thrift. 'The only thing that increases the actual wealth of the world is actual investment,' he continued, showing that the entrepreneurs, as innocent victims, cannot save themselves by making their workers victims too, via wage reductions and unemployment. Such a response, however rational by individual employers, has the effect of further reducing the purchasing power of the community below the level at which production is profitable. Admittedly, a cartel might help them avert a situation where everyone starves to death. Otherwise, he said, only two options remain: 'the thrift campaign falls off, or peters out. Or investment is increased.'[22]

Actually, the banana parable proves too much. Although it could be used to illustrate a downward multiplier effect, through decreased increments of spending, it still assumes that, if income is reduced, spending is also reduced by that whole amount. It overlooks the fact that savings will surely also be reduced under such circumstances – or, conversely, that savings will also be increased to some extent under circumstances where income is increasing. Others were ahead of Keynes in seeing the relevance of this point.

Keynes, however, did come to recognise the significance of the fact that changes in income will probably not produce exactly equal changes in consumption. He called it 'the psychological law that, when income increases, the gap between income and consumption will increase'. For if net personal savings increase in this way with increased prosperity, these savings will surely need to be matched by some commensurate increase in investment in order to sustain demand as a whole. A reorientation in Keynes's thinking during 1932 was prompted by his dawning realisation that orthodox theory had long ignored 'the theory of the demand and supply for output as a whole'.[23]

These were important stepping stones towards his own attempt to produce such a theory. As Keynes later put it: 'The novelty in my treatment of saving and investment consists, not in my maintaining their necessary aggregate equality, but in the proposition that it is, not the rate of interest, but the level of incomes which (in conjunction with certain other factors) ensures this equality.'[24] It follows that the level of output is itself the equilibrant, moving the economy between different positions, of which full employment is only one.

Then what role is left for interest rate? Not, any more, the key role that it had played in the *Treatise* and indeed all orthodox theory: that of the great equilibrant. There was now a gaping hole that Keynes needed to fill. He already had in his head his new theory of output as a whole when (as he once explained the process to Harrod) 'appreciably later, came the notion of interest as being the meaning of liquidity preference, which became quite clear in my mind the moment I thought of it'.[25] All those old discussions of 'bearishness', and 'hoarding' and 'the propensity to hoard', suddenly made a new kind of sense. He saw that everything turns on the psychology of the public about holding money itself, and thus on their reluctance to invest their savings when confidence collapses.

We can pinpoint when Keynes reached this crucial stage in his thinking – which was significantly earlier than used to be supposed. In the autumn of 1932, once every week for one university term, Keynes was giving his first lectures in Cambridge for two years. They were packed to the doors. Colleagues attended as well as undergraduates; but the graduate students kept the best notes. 'It was as if we were listening to Charles Darwin or Isaac Newton,' one American student recalled, no doubt mindful that these too were local heroes who had instigated far-reaching intellectual revolutions.[26] Keynes paid his audience the compliment of talking about the most interesting subject he could possibly imagine: his own new book, now in preparation.

The course was called 'The Monetary Theory of Production'. The notes of the graduate students for his fourth lecture, on 31 October 1932, show that Keynes led up to the conclusion that 'in itself the rate of interest is an expression of liquidity preference'.[27] So output as a whole was not in theory equilibrated by the interest rate; instead investment was the motor of the economy and the level of output the equilibrant. And at the end of term Keynes found a name for this far-reaching new analysis, after his friend Piero Sraffa had shown him the rediscovered correspondence to Ricardo from the combative Thomas Malthus, more than a century previously. Keynes decided to salute Malthus as yet another brave Cambridge pioneer by purloining his term 'effective demand' to describe his own theory of output as a whole.

Keynes had seized on the essentials of the theory of effective demand by the end of 1932. Thus girded, he went into battle; so when he almost immediately re-entered the ongoing polemics over economic policy, he did so backed by his new arguments. Until this point his practical proposals, although they might ring a bell with some Americans, were addressed to peculiarly British conditions, not readily applicable across the Atlantic. The United States was hardly the victim of the Gold Standard; the 'modus operandi of Bank rate' seemed foreign; the Treasury View was a construct of another people's Treasury. In 1933, by contrast, Keynes was ready to speak directly to the problems of Britain and the United States alike, with a new message which had a universal significance.

The author of the *Treatise* had been calling for stimulus measures for years. But, in theory, the *Treatise* had argued that flexible prices ought to deliver full employment. Keynes acknowledged time and again, to the Macmillan committee and elsewhere, the general principle that interest rates (or monetary policy) would do the trick. He said that cheap money could be relied upon to stimulate investment and thus economic recovery. The practical difficulty for Britain was simply that, under the Gold Standard, cheap money was not an option. Alternatively, it could be said that the British problem was sticky wages, which refused to respond to the credit squeeze of dear money by falling to an internationally competitive level. Unemployment was in this sense voluntary – collectively, workers chose to accept it rather than accept wage cuts. One way or another, these classical economic adjustments of the price level had failed to materialise; and Keynes had therefore opted for a series of second-best palliatives like tariffs and, above all, public works.

Keynes's maxim about the long run had particular pertinence under these conditions. It continued to provide a relevant test, but the conditions themselves changed. In 1931 Britain had gone off gold; the pound was no longer overvalued against the dollar; the special case of the *Treatise* was no longer operative.

The theoretical premise for his support for tariffs thus disappeared. Indeed Keynes at once abandoned this particular argument (though he still showed a hankering for home-grown solutions, as we have seen). Moreover, his special case for public works likewise disappeared, since the Bank of England no longer needed to maintain dear money. In fact, bank rate (or base rate), which had hovered around 5 per cent in the late 1920s, fell by June 1932 to 2 per cent and was to remain at that level until the eve of the Second World War. This was as low as the Bank of England had ever set its rate since its foundation in the late seventeenth century. Only in 2009 have we seen an even lower rate.

But cheap money did not do the trick – at least, not in Keynes's eyes. British unemployment remained historically high. Keynes consistently took the yardstick of 'normal' unemployment as about 5 per cent. The official figures in January 1933 showed a peak of 23 per cent.

If the interest rate could no longer be held responsible, perhaps the root of the problem, after all, might be uncompetitive wages in Britain. This was broadly the conclusion that Hubert Henderson had reached in 1930–1. At that point, when Keynes was accused by his old comrade of evading the remedy of 'an assault on wages', he could only respond that 'I twist and turn about' in seeking alternatives, because an increase in investment rather than a reduction in wages still seemed more promising.[28] There is indeed a good argument for saying that high costs, including labour costs, made British prices uncompetitive in world terms, even if Keynes himself – like Pigou – was reluctant to see wage reductions as a practical remedy. But this too changed once the whole world spiralled into Depression, with unemployment rising in practically every country. How could all countries be simultaneously uncompetitive with each other? How could wage cuts, in all countries simultaneously, help the overall situation?

Orthodox economists, like Pigou, could well persist in the view that 'gadgets' and 'devices' were still in practice necessary. What now distinguished Keynes was that, for the first time, he approached the problem with a *theory* that challenged orthodoxy. Monetary policy was no longer Keynes's theoretical remedy. Yes, it could do the trick of checking inflationary exuberance, rather like pulling on a piece of string. But this was its only trick. Faced with the actual depressed, deflationary problem of the 1930s, it was like pushing on a piece of string. Rock-bottom interest rates failed to deliver the necessary stimulus.

Keynes now moved with such confidence because of intellectual conviction. The members of the Circus shared his thrilling sense of discovering inherent truths rather than inventing tactical arguments. The new book that he was writing was plainly not going to revise the *Treatise* but supersede it altogether. As he later told the story to Harrod, although there was 'an immense lot of muddling and many drafts' necessary to make it fit for publication, it was the change in his thinking during 1932 that produced 'the moments of transition which were for me personally moments of illumination' – glimpsing 'particles of light in escaping from a tunnel'.[29]

The theory of effective demand now explained that an equilibrium had indeed been achieved between saving and investment. But it was an equilibrium at less than full employment. Individual action was powerless to achieve results that could be secured only through collective action. Hence the new relevance of a stimulus package, whether at home or abroad, in one country or – preferably – the whole world. Although the term equilibrium had a comforting ring, suggesting that the economy was in balance, the real implication was sinister. The economy was at rest. It was not self-righting.

Here was Keynes's revolution: one prompted by his engagement with real-world economic policy debates but transcending them with an analysis that changed the paradigm. The analysis, moreover, was already operational three years before the *General Theory* was published. His subsequent toils in drafting the book were not wasted, not unduly slow, not particularly easy, not unnecessary in providing the tight formal demonstrations that would convince the 'fellow economists' to whom the book was addressed. But his work here was more than that of embellishing a few technical or mathematical propositions with suitable rhetoric, applied afterwards for effect – if anything, the other way round. 'The precise use of language comes at a late stage in the development of one's thoughts,' said Keynes in one of his university lectures. 'You can think accurately and effectively long before you can so to speak photograph your thought.'[30]

From the beginning of 1933, after nearly a year and a half of relative public silence, Keynes energetically began to publicise his new thinking. There was a new fiscal emphasis, consistent with his own shift away from monetary policy. In Britain, the National Government's attempts to balance the budget at the bottom of a slump were his immediate target. In a radio broadcast, he insisted that 'you will never balance the Budget through measures which reduce the national income'. Cuts in government spending, especially unemployment benefits, were thus self-defeating. 'Look after the unemployment, and the Budget will look after itself' was the new watchword. Indeed he went so far as to say that 'the Chancellor of the Exchequer would be long-sighted if he were to take rather an optimistic view, and give us perhaps in his next Budget rather more relief than is strictly justified by the facts actually in sight'.[31]

For those who automatically associate the name of Keynes with budget deficits, these remarks may seem curiously tepid. None the less they are virtually the only endorsement he ever gave to running a fiscal deficit on current account. What he actually wanted was still loan-financed capital projects, for the obvious reason that this was a direct stimulus to investment. This was naturally the thrust of his proposals in his important and well-publicised pamphlet 'The Means to Prosperity', the American edition of which, in April 1933, incorporated his first published exposition of the multiplier.

Keynes was now, of course, in a position to give more robust answers to two long-standing objections. He could specify the cumulative effect of public works upon employment; and he could explain where the money was to be found. 'Just as an initial impulse of modest dimensions has been capable of producing such devastating repercussions, so also a moderate impulse in the opposite direction will effect a surprising recovery,' he wrote in the American edition of 'Means to Prosperity'. He acknowledged the unfamiliarity of the new ideas that he was seeking to popularise, but insisted that the old theories were irrelevant: 'Many people are trying to solve the problem of unemployment with a theory which is based on the assumption that there is no unemployment.'[32]

Persuasion seemed more crucial than ever. Keynes's own task in persuading inside opinion was a prelude to the persuasion of outside opinion. The psychology of the public fed into market confidence, with effects that were often self-fulfilling. Roosevelt's inaugural address in March 1933 was famous for the claim that there was nothing to fear but fear itself. Perhaps too much time has been spent in scrutinising the possible influence of Keynes on Roosevelt; perhaps instead the influence of Roosevelt on Keynes needs more recognition. At any rate, in the following month,

Keynes furnished a congenially similar message in a British context, as usual criticising Neville Chamberlain as Chancellor of the Exchequer. 'Unfortunately the more pessimistic the Chancellor's policy, the more likely it is that pessimistic anticipations will be

President Franklin D. Roosevelt's inauguration in March 1933, when he said that there was nothing to fear but fear itself.

realised and vice versa,' said Keynes. 'Whatever the Chancellor dreams, will come true!'[33] The new President's dreams were more like his own.

If we want to know why a car is sometimes driving safely along the road, but sometimes crashes or breaks down, we have alternative ways of explaining it. One explanation is mechanical, showing the necessary effects of engine capacity and efficiency in determining the engine's exact performance limits. The other explanation concentrates on the human factor, exploring the judgement of the driver in making decisions that may well be subject to external distraction or temperamental readiness to take risks. The theory of effective demand, as conceived in 1932, was more like the first kind of analysis. It was essentially hydraulic, specifying necessary flows and displacements, just as the modus operandi of bank rate, though working in a different way, had also been hydraulic.

What about the *General Theory* itself, as published in 1936? In protracted revision of drafts of the book, it took on a further dimension, infused with more subjective notions, not only about psychology but uncertainty too. In the process, Keynes was returning to ideas that he had first broached a quarter of a century earlier, in his work on probability, as we saw in Chapter 1. He was also, of course, picking up themes from A *Treatise on Money*, reformulating insights about the role of expectations. Many early Keynesians – and there was none earlier than James Meade – saw no contradiction in taking expectations as given, then specifying determinate results for the system.

Few economists would disagree that Keynes played a key role in establishing the importance of macroeconomics. Although the term itself was not used until the 1940s, and never by Keynes himself, the study of the system *as a whole* surely informs his approach. Citation counts in economic journals of the period show that the *Treatise* had already made Keynes the world's most cited macroeconomist, displacing the American Irving Fisher. After the *General Theory*, Keynes's primacy was unrivalled. His name was cited nearly three times more often than the next-ranking economist (Dennis Robertson), four times more often than Pigou, five times more often than Harrod, Hawtrey or Hayek, six times more often than Joan Robinson, eight times more often than Ohlin and nine times more often than Schumpeter.[34]

The structure of the *General Theory* makes clear why this is so. It is divided into six parts. The first concludes by rejecting the direction taken by classical economics since Malthus – a huge and provocative claim, of course. As Keynes privately told Harrod: 'I want, so to speak, to raise a dust; because it is only out of the controversy that will arise that what I am saying will get understood.'[35] This helps explain the sharpness of the distinctions made in expounding the theory of effective demand in the early parts of the book.

If aggregate output is to find a market, and thus make production profitable, there must be an equivalent amount of aggregate demand. Effective demand comprises both consumption and investment. Both of them are the product of active choices or decisions – unlike saving, which is a passive residual. (So Marshall's argument that saving is simply deferred spending has to be dismissed.) Therefore the part of current income that is *not* spent on consumption goods must be matched by investment, which is itself spending on capital goods. Otherwise there will be disabling repercussions.

Individual choice in a free market is real. Or rather, the initial decision is real but the overall outcome might be unintended and perverse. For saving and investment are only reconciled in aggregate by changes in income. Saving, like spending, is a two-sided affair. One person's consumption is another person's income; one person's thrift can be another person's loss of income. Saving, as a product of the collective behaviour of consumers, will necessarily be brought into equality with investment, as a product of the collective behaviour of entrepreneurs. This has to be so since each of them, saving and investment alike, equals income minus consumption.

There will thus be an equilibrium, of sorts. It will not, however, necessarily be at full employment or optimal output, since it is aggregate output itself that will have to accommodate – producing any level of income or output or employment that will equilibrate saving and investment. The final words of the book's second part point to 'the vital difference between the theory of the economic behaviour of the aggregate and the theory of the behaviour of the individual unit, in which we assume that changes in the individual's own demand do not affect his income'.[36]

The third part of the *General Theory*, 'The propensity to consume', draws together vital parts of the argument. 'The ultimate object of our analysis is to discover what determines the volume of employment,' Keynes writes; and his key suggestion is that it is the aggregate demand function that has been overlooked.[37] Since demand comprises both investment and consumption, both are necessary. It was nothing new for Keynes to stress the key role of investment. But the analysis of the *General Theory*, in concentrating on the 'propensity to consume' rather than the disposition to save, gives a new twist to the argument. In principle, deficient consumption might, as much as deficient investment, be called the root of the problem, since both stem from attempts to save too much. This third part of the book concludes by calling unemployment 'the inevitable result of applying to the conduct of the State the maxims which are best calculated to "enrich" an individual ...'[38]

Here is the famous paradox of thrift. It is a paradox because it seems natural to suppose that if individual saving enriches the individual concerned, it must also enrich the community. 'The error lies in proceeding to the plausible inference that, when an individual saves, he will increase aggregate investment by an equal amount,' the *General Theory* tells us.[39] It was a story that Keynes had told before, as in the banana parable, with excessive thrift promoting an inadvertent spiral of declining prices, declining profits, declining employment, declining incomes, declining prosperity all round. His account – now more cogent and more coherent – turns on the distinction between what is true for individuals and what is true in aggregate.

Keynes was not the first person in history to have seized on this crucial insight. In the *General Theory* he is very generous in dispensing acknowledgements to pioneers who had preceded him in identifying the paradox of thrift. In Chapter 23, he has enormous fun in rehabilitating a whole gallery of economic heretics, especially Bernard de Mandeville for his early-eighteenth-century *Fable of the Bees*, and, of course, Malthus, on whom he had already published a biographical essay. There is also a seven-page tribute to J. A. Hobson, best remembered now for his pioneering analysis of imperialism and best known at that time for his propositions about 'under-consumption'. Hobson in his old age was obviously deeply gratified to hear that his work represented 'an epoch in economic thought'.[40]

Keynes actually learnt little from Hobson – but should have learnt more. The *General Theory* was already in proof before the section on Hobson was drafted with Kahn's help. Hobson was a freelance intellectual who had never held any professorial post in Britain, though he was an honoured visitor to American universities, notably the University of Wisconsin, where his kind of 'progressive' political commitments struck a common chord. He had been closer to Keynes ideologically rather than academically. True, Hobson and Keynes had both come to focus on an aggregate process that could be called over-saving; but for Hobson, taking saving and investment as the same activity, this meant over-investment, with the only remedy an increase in consumption; whereas for Keynes, of course, over-saving meant under-investment, and stimulating investment was the key. The *General Theory* tactfully brings out this difference, while hailing Hobson as an 'economic heretic' who deserved better than the slights of the economic profession.

What Keynes ignored, however, was a Hobsonian insight that he could well have picked up sooner. For Hobson identified his own (valid) contentions about the fatuity of collective over-saving as 'at root a very simple fallacy, viz. the contention that what anyone can do, all can do'.[41] Hobson called this the individualist fallacy and a favourite illustration was to say that although it might be true that any boy could go from a log cabin to the White House, not all could do so simultaneously.

This idea is sometime called the fallacy of composition. Its centrality can hardly be exaggerated, since it is, in a sense, the general theory behind the *General Theory*. For example, there cannot be any actual aggregate of excess savings: it is an excessive *propensity* to save that produces the perverse effects. Keynes sees that each of us individually may try to execute strategies that appear rational to ourselves. But these may prove self-defeating if we all try at once. Yet we can all see, in principle, what would be in our collective self-interest. So there are intractable theoretical reasons why market failure can leave us impotent to achieve what we actually want – unless, that is, government can intervene to save us.

There is a second guiding insight at the heart of Keynes's intellectual revolution. This harks back to his earliest academic work, on probability. He put this best in an article that he wrote at the end of 1936 for the Harvard University *Quarterly Journal of Economics*, called 'The general theory of employment'. Here, uncertainty emerges as the ghost in the Keynesian machine. He suggests that 'the fact that our knowledge of the future is fluctuating, vague and uncertain, renders wealth a peculiarly unsuitable subject for the methods of the classical political economy'. He sees that, while we can estimate *probabilities*, however remote, when faced with *uncertainty*, we move beyond the reach of scientific calculation. 'We simply do not know,' Keynes tells us. Yet it is a world pervaded by uncertainty in which we live, and have to make decisions every day, economic decisions not least. So 'our desire to hold money as a store of wealth is a barometer of the degree of our distrust of our own calculations and conventions concerning the future'.[42]

Expectations are thus the key. And that necessarily means what we expect from a viewpoint that is before the event. Whether expectations are rational depends on whether they are based on reasonable judgment exercised *ex ante*, not on how this appears *ex post*. If we apply such thinking to the economy today, then, we can see obvious objections to any model of 'rational expectations' that defines rationality as the market behaviour that is actually fulfilled. At any rate, the application of 'rational expectations' to license a view of the market as omniscient seems rather naive.

Our decisions may not be irrational, but to suppose that our expectations can be totally rational is a fallacy. The economy depends on investment, and investment depends on expectations, however limited in their scientific basis. The *General Theory* itself makes this very clear. 'It would be foolish, in forming our expectations, to attach great weight to matters which are very uncertain,' it warns us, invoking the *Treatise on Probability*.[43] The precariousness of our knowledge is one theme, the pragmatic response of falling back upon convention another. Second-guessing the psychology of the market itself becomes the motive force. 'Speculators may do no harm as bubbles on a steady stream of enterprise,' allowed Keynes, letting himself off lightly before reproaching Wall Street in particular: 'When the capital development of a country becomes a by-product of the activities of a casino, the job is likely to be ill-done.'[44]

This is partly an institutional problem, in stacking market incentives in the wrong way. But human nature itself cannot be ignored. Confidence is crucial to expectations; the future depends upon its robustness; yet it is far from rational. 'Most, probably, of our decisions to do something positive, the full consequences of which will be drawn out over many days to come, can only be taken as a result of animal spirits – of a spontaneous urge to action rather than inaction, and not as the outcome of a weighted average of quantitative benefits multiplied by quantitative probabilities.'[45] Keynes's pregnant reference to animal spirits did not, unfortunately, give birth to a more extensive analysis of market expectations, though it certainly pointed to the need for one.

The *General Theory* is not a handbook of economic policy. Though its insights can be applied to particular conditions, its essential claims are universal. When an increasingly sceptical Robertson told Keynes in 1935 that he thought that much of the theoretical structure was mumbo-jumbo, Keynes responded sharply that 'this book is a purely theoretical work, *not* a collection of wisecracks. *Everything* turns on the mumbo-jumbo ...'[46] Unlike the *Treatise*, which had special reference to Britain as an open economy, subject to external forces, the *General Theory* applies in principle to a closed economy, just as the whole world is by definition a closed economy.

'I have called my theory a *general* theory,' Keynes wrote in the preface to the French edition. 'I mean by this that I am chiefly concerned with the behaviour of the economic system as a whole, – with aggregate incomes, aggregate profits, aggregate output, aggregate employment, aggregate investment, aggregate saving rather than the incomes, profits, output, employment, investment and saving of particular industries, firms or individuals.'[47] Maybe he believed this at the moment when he put it quite like that; but the real reason why Keynes hit on this name for his book was surely that, with a nod towards Albert Einstein, whom he had met and admired, he wanted to claim its general status as opposed to a special theory, valid only under certain conditions.

Keynes was enough of an intellectual magpie himself not to spoil the sport of other magpies, stealing bright ideas. He was determined not to be possessive about insights that he readily acknowledged he had adapted from others. But he was clearly worried about attempts to assimilate selected aspects of his thinking into orthodox economic theory, as a special case. Thus the multiplier could be accepted – but not the equilibration of saving and investment via output changes. Or liquidity preference could be accepted – but not as the replacement of the traditional theory of interest, only as an interesting modification. So the Keynesian revolution might well be marginalised as a sub-species of 'depression economics', dependent on the rigidity of wages and a peculiar 'liquidity trap' that temporarily thwarted the proper workings of interest rate. But he envisaged a system that was symmetrical: in principle able to cope with the danger of inflation once full employment was reached.

By the forbidding standards of most treatises on theoretical economics, the *General Theory* is a good read. 'The ideas which are here expressed so laboriously are extremely simple and should be obvious,' says the preface.[48] Keynes claimed to be writing in a relatively technical way only because his fellow economists needed a professionally thorough de-bamboozling. For himself, he had no doubts that his own escape from his Marshallian education had been psychological as much as intellectual. As he told his unpersuaded friend Dennis Robertson in 1937, 'I am trying all the time to disentangle myself, whilst you are trying to keep entangled.' Hence Keynes's exhilaration, once he believed that he had accomplished his revolution in economic theory – 'I am shaking myself like a dog on dry land.'[49] He spoke in Stockholm about the *General Theory* shortly after its publication. 'What I have to say intrinsically easy,' read his lecture notes, characteristically adding: 'It is only to an audience of economists that it is difficult.'[50]

Epilogue
British and American Keynesianism

THERE IS MUCH talk today about the end of an epoch in Anglo-American economic policy. 'Since Bretton Woods, the world has been living on a financial model, the Anglo-Saxon model,' said the French President, Nicolas Sarkozy, happy to salute the G20 meeting in April 2009 as instead turning a new page. The British Prime Minister, Gordon Brown, claimed that this G20 summit marked the end of the 'Washington consensus'.[1] In international finance, to be sure, we are saying goodbye to some of the assumptions that Keynes made about the postwar world, especially his dated preconception that the English-speaking peoples had an innate destiny and competence – a sort of economic analogue to Churchill's claims about Britain's special relationship with the United States. Conversely, interest has revived in plans like 'Bancor' and a genuinely reciprocal role for the nations comprising the IMF, much along lines that Keynes himself initially suggested.

In domestic economic policy, few now repeat the dismissive taunt of the 1980s, that the ideas of Keynes are dead and buried. Again, this is a perspective with a particular Anglo-American relevance. The economic policies of Reagan's America and Thatcher's Britain were premised on a rejection of the 'Keynesian consensus' of the 1960s. Moreover, this right-wing agenda in turn shaped a new non-Keynesian Anglo-American consensus – unchallenged in its essentials by the Democrats under Bill Clinton or New Labour under Tony Blair. Globalisation, free markets and light-touch regulation became the slogans of an era in which the financial sector stoked runaway growth and unbounded market euphoria. Wall Street and the City of London were the pace-setters, at least in financial recklessness. Little wonder, now that boom has turned to gloom, that it is particularly in the United States and Britain that the reputation of the defunct economist is again riding the roller-coaster. We are reminded every week of the relevance of Keynesian insights that seemed to have been discredited a quarter of a century ago.

Keynes wrote the *General Theory* about the whole world and for the whole world. It thus dealt with the economic system as a whole; he hoped to proselytize across frontiers. To French readers he felt it necessary to offer an explicit word of explanation about his own education in a peculiarly English kind of economic orthodoxy: 'I learnt it, I taught it, I wrote it.'[2] But France, with its tradition of *l'état tutélaire* rather than principled laissez-faire, did not need to be disabused of these classical fallacies. Keynesian ideas simply did not offer French intellectuals the sort of frisson in challenging established conventions that young British and American converts experienced. Since the French, unlike the Anglo-Saxons, had always taken the state for granted, much in the Keynesian analysis seemed mere common sense. After the Liberation in 1944 it could be said with a shrug that being a Keynesian 'was a polite way of being a socialist'.[3] Real socialists knew better, realising that Keynes was no socialist and fearing that he might be the saviour of reformed capitalism.

There were translations of the *General Theory* into Spanish, Czech, Italian, Serbo-Croat, Hindi, Finnish, Romanian, Hungarian and Russian as well as French, German and Japanese. Like the French edition, the German and Japanese translations each had a separate preface. In both of these, Keynes likewise felt the need to explain why his self-proclaimed economic heresy seemed so shocking to English readers. He acknowledged that 'all this may impress German readers somewhat differently'; he admitted that 'Japanese readers, however, will neither require nor resist my assaults against the English tradition'.[4] He was correct in supposing that the bold colours of revolution in which he draped his new doctrine would look rather pale in countries that were already long habituated to spontaneous co-ordination through the institutions of civil society.

These were, of course, tendencies that fed into authoritarian models of government in the 1930s. It came as no surprise that both imperial Japan and Nazi Germany administered an ongoing government stimulus to their economies, and did so by appealing to a highly traditional military rationale. Here Keynesianism as such made relatively little impression – either before or immediately after the Second World War. In Italy, where supporters of the Mussolini regime had sometimes appropriated Keynesian ideas about public expenditure, liberal economists remained suspicious of *'il Piano Keynes'* – one Keynes Plan too many. Instead, Luigi Einaudi purported to champion the 'common man' who knew perfectly well that investment required prior savings and that 'one cannot make hare pie without the hare'.[5] It was Einaudi who was to shape the country's economic policy, to serve as Minister of Finance after the war and as President of the republic from 1948 to 1955. He was backed by the political mobilisation of the postwar Christian Democrats, confident that any Keynes boom was already over, and determined to ignore Italian Keynesians. Such examples show how idiosyncratically Keynes was 'translated'.

The American edition of the *General Theory*, however, was exactly the same as the English edition, and for a very good reason. It was not just that Americans spoke English: many in the American elite subscribed to a political culture shared by the English-speaking peoples, broadly accepting the naturalness of a liberal, free-market economic order. (This was also true of Canada, Australia and New Zealand.) The classical orthodoxy of a self-adjusting system based on sound money and balanced budgets was thus entrenched within a common Anglo-American tradition. Keynes had learnt this, he had taught it, he had written it – and he exaggerated it. For he was actually oblivious of some important differences between American and British political culture that were to make Keynesianism in the United States distinctive, and arguably unfaithful to his intentions.

Joseph Schumpeter, as so often, had a trenchant opinion that is worth serious consideration. In his generous obituary notice in 1946, he warned that 'Keynes's advice was in the first instance always English advice, born of English problems even where addressed to other nations'. No reader of the *Treatise* would fail to see the point of this remark, still less would any American wartime negotiator, listening to Lord Keynes's beguilingly helpful suggestions about why it was in the United States's own best interests to supply Britain freely with yet more fat wads of dollars. But Schumpeter's claim, if true, has broader implications. It reflects his own understanding of Keynes's thinking, allegedly proceeding in a straight line from *The Economic Consequences of the Peace* to the *General Theory*, as a sort of vast rationalisation of Britain's economic decline and loss of buoyancy. How unlike the vibrant process of 'creative destruction' that Schumpeter saw embodied in American capitalism! Hence his judgement that 'practical Keynesianism is a seedling which cannot be transplanted into foreign soil: it dies there and becomes poisonous before it dies'.[6]

This book has given a wholly different account of Keynes's intellectual trajectory. In particular it has demonstrated the significance of the theoretical break between the fundamentally orthodox vision that Keynes maintained up to the *Treatise* and the new thinking of the *General Theory*. The grain of truth in

Schumpeter's version is none the less worthy of attention: that we should not be surprised to find differences between American and British Keynesianism. Like an American remake of a popular British television series, though the basic storyline might sound familiar, there have also been some remarkable departures from the original in adapting to transatlantic susceptibilities.

A common language makes it easy to underestimate differences between British and American governance, which seem initially so easy to allow for. For President, read Prime Minister; for Congress, read Parliament; for Federal Reserve Board (FRB), read Bank of England; for Republican, read Conservative; for Democrat, read Liberal or Labour; and so on. Yet, here too, much is lost in translation. And such terms as Cabinet, Treasury or legislative process, which hardly seem to need translation at all, can lead to misconceptions when the same word is applied to such different effect on either side of the Atlantic. Keynes often transferred to the United States some typically British assumptions: that 'the authorities' would surely act in concert, that the government of the day would always get its way, that 'inside opinion' spoke with one voice, and that a well-drilled Civil Service would seamlessly implement consistent, agreed policies. Roosevelt's Washington, in particular, was simply not like this.

Other contrasts with Britain reflect obvious differences between the size and nature and openness of the two economies. The economic history of the United States could be seen as an interaction between a continually expanding frontier and exponential population growth, together producing endless opportunities for investment in the heroic task of developing the infrastructure of half a continent. In the twentieth century, however, with the frontier closed and immigration checked, what was to prevent stagnation setting in? In this perspective, the First World War itself and its backlog of reconstruction provided strictly temporary reasons for the American boom of the 1920s. But what next? The collapse after 1929 looked all the more serious, prospects of natural recovery seemed all the more unlikely – even in the long run.

This perspective was essentially that of Professor Alvin Hansen. A South Dakota farm boy, only four years younger than Keynes, and for a long time sceptical of his theories, Hansen eventually arrived at Harvard in a senior position in 1937, a year after the *General Theory* had already made its mark there. Hansen became its most influential American convert. The start of his academic career had been at the University of Wisconsin, under Professor Richard T. Ely, the leading American sponsor of J. A. Hobson's economic theories; and the ideas of the American under-consumptionists, William Foster and Waddill Catchings, though even less academically respectable than those of Hobson, were also familiar to Hansen. Like Keynes in Cambridge, Hansen, once established in the other Cambridge, was in a position to put a prestigious institutional imprimatur upon notions that might otherwise have been dismissed as populist heresies, peddled only by cranks.

One outcome, in the American policy debates of the late 1930s, was a new stress upon maintaining consumption as well as investment. It was Hansen who thus gave Keynesianism a home-grown American twist, using his year as president of the American Economic Association in 1938 to promulgate the word. The message was that any effect of New Deal expenditures in putting the budget into deficit should be welcomed rather than feared, perpetuated rather than quickly reversed, since 'secular stagnation stalks across the stage, or at least shows its face'.[7] This doctrine, for better or worse, should be attributed to Hansen rather than directly to Keynes, who at most hinted at such possibilities.

The New Deal has always had a reputation as an era of high government spending. But the United States federal budgets, especially in the late 1930s, tell a rather different story. Roosevelt, albeit encumbered by much of his own campaign rhetoric denouncing Hoover as a spendthrift, indeed initiated programmes that widened the deficit until 1936. But total federal spending in these years, itself never more than 6 per cent of GNP, was often counteracted in its stimulative effects by cutbacks at state or local levels. Such net effects would today be considered far too small to pull the country out of a Depression that left a minimum of 14 per cent unemployed – and was to take unemployment back up to 19 per cent in 1937–8.[8]

Through Keynesian spectacles, the reason for the recession that interrupted recovery in 1937 looked clear as soon as it happened. Keynes wrote privately that 'it should have been obvious that, as soon as the Government began spending less, and as soon as the pace of improvement was somewhat moderated, a set back was inevitable'.[9] The recession, in fact, was the result of a misguided

Henry Morgenthau, Roosevelt's long-serving Treasury Secretary, closeted with Keynes during their wartime negotiations.

plan by the Treasury Secretary, Henry Morgenthau, to balance the budget by 1938. Morgenthau's old crony in the Hudson River squirearchy, Roosevelt himself, had been ready to go along with this scheme, as usual heavily influenced by the supposed political advantages, in this case in painting the Republicans as the party of profligacy. Instead, the reality was that the Democrats, rather than using the New Deal to champion workers fearful of losing their jobs, were painting themselves into a corner.

It was to be justifiably dubbed 'the Roosevelt recession'. Keynes already knew that 'the President himself has been content with general notions, a conduit pipe for the more general ideas of others', as he had put it in 1934.[10] He had a personal meeting with the President later that year, leaving it more impressed with Roosevelt's political instinct than his economic grasp. When Keynes was later in Washington, representing Churchill's wartime government, he observed that the President was not at his best on 'the pressing and difficult details of economic policy, which he does not really care for any more than our own Prime Minister does'.[11] The 1937 budget judgement certainly bears this out. Roosevelt, for his part, had robustly told Schumpeter at the time: 'I am compelled to admit – or boast – whichever way you care to put it, that I know nothing of economics and that nobody else does either!'[12] But he knew enough about politics to see that, with the 1938 congressional elections looming, the Democrats were better-off looking after their natural constituency than point-scoring about a budget record that produced such perverse effects.

Here was the opportunity for the American Keynesians to score a decisive triumph. When Hansen testified before a key congressional committee in early 1939, he was supported in his advice by Lauchlin Currie, a younger economist with a Harvard pedigree and now a key presidential adviser. Their argument, that a budget deficit was necessary in order to stimulate effective demand, this time carried the day. As Currie put it in a memorandum for the President in March 1940: 'The basic analysis is that of J. M. Keynes.'[13] It is indisputable that US fiscal policy now took the expansionary turn which was to be sustained until the end of the Second World War; indisputable too that unemployment at last fell as the war economy boomed. As we have already seen, Keynes himself naturally welcomed 'expenditure on the scale necessary to make the grand experiments which would prove my case'.[14]

But things are not quite so simple. The case that Keynes had long made, of course, was for public works, as a necessary stimulus to an under-performing economy because what was needed was more *investment*. Currie appreciated this perfectly well, having written in a review of the *General Theory* that it was 'a peculiarity of Keynes's work that he appears always to think of an increase in income as being generated by an increase in investment and never by an increase in consumption'.[15] Yet what Currie used his influence to push across the President's desk was a supposedly Keynesian proposal based on increasing *consumption*. Currie, by now hardened to the ways of the White House, knew perfectly well what he was doing here. As he later confessed, 'I referred to the basic analysis as Keynesian but it is possible I thought this would make it more acceptable.'[16] This is, of course, itself a tribute to the power that Keynes's name had acquired by this point.

The broader point is that American Keynesianism became identified with a fiscal strategy that used the budget to manipulate consumption levels. It was quite natural that fiscal policy should have had this priority for the administration in the 1930s, if only because it was directly under the control of the White House. The United States historically lacked the sort of central bank that most countries take for granted. The American monetary system thus remained relatively decentralised, with twelve federal reserve banks exercising appreciable autonomy, until – discredited by the Depression – the system was reformed in 1935. Only then did the Federal Reserve Board in Washington acquire undisputed primacy. Even then, lacking the sort of co-ordination with Treasury policy that was axiomatic for the Bank of England, there remained a striking contrast with the venerable authority and cohesion of 'the authorities' in London. Thus there are long-standing institutional reasons why the United States did not see a tighter co-ordination of monetary and fiscal policy, such as was customary in Britain.

The fiscal emphasis of American Keynesianism was one immediate result. In the long run, it was to reinforce the knee-jerk association of Keynesianism with budget deficits and 'tax-and-spend' policies. Even in Keynes's own lifetime, it became apparent to him that the bevy of American disciples whom he encountered on his wartime visits to the United States had an agenda that often differed from his own, at least in emphasis and tactics. The *General Theory*, just as its author had predicted to Bernard Shaw, was to be mixed with politics and passions in the course of its reception by the world. Keynes was enough of a pragmatist, enough of an opportunist, not to quibble. After dining with a group of American Keynesian economists in Washington, DC, in 1944, Keynes said at breakfast the next morning: 'I was the only non-Keynesian there.'[17]

We might reasonably expect British Keynesianism to have been more faithful to Keynes's own ideas. During his lifetime, this is broadly true. His own policy interventions after the *General Theory* had been published provide our best guide to the thinking of the historical Keynes. After 1946, admittedly, Keynesianism became a handy label on both sides of the Atlantic for policies that were readily ascribed to a posthumous Keynes – or sometimes to an apocryphal Keynes.

If there is one thing that everyone knows about Keynes, it is surely that he favoured budget deficits. This is his political legacy – or so we have been assured on the authority of the Nobel laureate James Buchanan, notably in the influential book that he published with Richard E. Wagner, *Democracy in Deficit* (1977). The eager student who supposes that Keynes wrote of little else may resort to the short cut of using the cumulative index to the magnificent Royal Economic Society edition, in all its twenty-nine volumes, of Keynes's collected writings. Yes, budget deficits are certainly there, taking up five lines of the index, or one-tenth of one column out of 746. The fact that, for about 99.9 per cent of the time, Keynes was evidently *not* writing about deficits will seem surprising only to those – including many famous economists today – who have never actually read any of his books.

In the *General Theory*, there are only two direct references to budget deficits. One is almost an aside, to the effect that a slump will be mitigated if the government, 'willingly or unwillingly', tolerates a deficit through its expenditure on unemployment relief payments.[18] It is true that, although British folk memory is of a miserly 'dole' paid to workers who lost their jobs during the slump, the level of government support for the unemployed in Britain was high by international standards – certainly in comparison with the United States. And we now know that Keynes was correct in thinking that this made the impact of the Depression in Britain relatively less severe. What Keynes was against was a self-defeating attempt to balance the budget in a recession by cuts that would inadvertently prolong it rather than achieve their professed objective.

The other relevant passage in the *General Theory* is more extensive. Here Keynes is defending what he usually calls 'loan expenditure' by government when faced with mass unemployment. This is the perennial argument about the Treasury View: whether government is simply robbing an equivalent sum of private investment in a way that therefore seems 'wasteful' unless government is better able than private enterprise to choose the right projects. But Keynes's argument, of course, is that a net stimulus is applied by mobilising resources that are otherwise unemployed. So the stimulative effect comes irrespective of the utility of the particular project. 'Pyramid-building, earthquakes, even wars may serve to increase wealth, if the education of our statesmen on the principles of the classical economics stands in the way of anything better.' Hence his satirical defence – taken rather literally by some critics – of digging holes in the ground, rather than doing nothing (though it would, he solemnly adds, 'be more sensible to build houses and the like').[19]

Explicit references to deficits in Keynes's writings in fact come mainly in an American context. Thus in 1934 he defended Roosevelt's expenditure on public works and unemployment relief, creating 'the enormous so-called deficit – much of which, however, will be covered by valuable assets'.[20] Keynes certainly approved of loan expenditure of this kind; and he extended this approval to consumption once he had the multiplier concept clear. 'Spending is a two-sided transaction,' he wrote at the end of 1934, anticipating the arguments of the *General Theory* that it increases incomes all round. 'The predominant issue, as I look at the matter,' he told his American readers, 'is to get the money spent.'[21]

During the Second World War, Keynes was himself in the government service in Britain. By then, under American influence, the terms 'deficit finance' and 'functional finance' had become established. Some of the younger Keynesian economists working for the British government were much taken with such ideas and began arguing for the postwar regulation of demand through consumption. This would mean running deficits by cutting taxes in a recession. Keynes, however, continued to argue in favour of public investment in the infrastructure, preferably through instituting a 'capital budget' to finance it, while leaving the ordinary budget in balance. He advised the Chancellor of the Exchequer to avoid 'confusing the fundamental idea of the capital budget with the particular, rather desperate expedient of deficit financing'.[22]

Keynes conducted fascinating arguments on how to maintain full employment with his younger friend James Meade, now also working as a government economist. Meade was at this point more like an American Keynesian in countenancing deficit finance, arguing that tax cuts could provide a more immediate stimulus than public works. Keynes, by contrast, was sceptical whether taxpayers would vary their spending in the necessary manner. 'People have established standards of life,' he cautioned Meade. 'Nothing will upset them more than to be subject to pressure constantly to vary them up and down. A remission of taxation on which people could only rely for an indefinitely short period might have very limited effects in stimulating their consumption.'[23] When Milton Friedman made similar points, arguing that people related their spending to their 'permanent' income, his concept of the stability of the consumption function rightly received recognition in the late 1950s. It is piquant to find Keynes telling some of this to Meade in 1943.

Keynes made one concession towards stimulating consumption, rather than his usual preferred alternative of stimulating investment. This was to endorse Meade's idea for regulating the level of National Insurance payments. These were the contributions paid by British workers and their employers into the state-subsidised fund that guaranteed a right to unemployment relief payments for those out of work. It was the inability of the National Insurance fund itself to meet such payments during the Depression, and the consequent need to bail it out, that had put a strain on the budget in the early 1930s – the one form of deficit that Keynes happily welcomed as counter-cyclical in its effect. Meade had the idea of extending this principle in plans for postwar reconstruction, by levying higher rates of contributions during economic booms and cutting them when the economy was in recession. Although never implemented, this proposal had Keynes's support and was, he argued, 'not open to many of the objections to other forms of deficit finance'.[24]

Keynes had addressed the deflationary problems of the slump in the 1930s and the *General Theory* naturally reflects this concern. It had focused on the insufficiency of effective demand to sustain employment, whereas the war economy presented wholly different problems. If the analysis of the *General Theory* had simply been an exercise in depression economics, its author might modestly have put it aside – at least until the next depression.

Instead, of course, he demonstrated its essentially symmetrical nature by coming up with another Keynes Plan. *How to Pay for the War* (1940) is thus an adaptation of the same macroeconomic analysis to an economy in which the problem is no longer that of tackling deflation and unemployment but of warding off the equal and opposite dangers of inflation and labour shortage. The war economy legitimised stimulus measures, notably loan-financed increases in public spending, with government orders bringing much of manufacturing industry into full production for the first time in years. It was only logical, therefore, that Keynes's plan should have been addressed to restraining the prospective inflationary effect, by expedients that would take excess consuming power out of the economy. To this end, he proposed not only high levels of progressive taxation but measures for 'deferred pay' – in effect a temporary withholding tax, to be credited to payers of income tax after the war. Despite initial opposition from the Labour movement, a scaled-down version was to be introduced in 1941.

Under these new conditions, what a Keynesian policy meant was the use of the budget to check inflation. Indeed this shift of priorities had already been signalled in Keynes's pre-war advice, once signs of economic recovery became intermittently apparent in Britain, as in the United States. 'Just as it was advisable for the Government to incur debt during the slump,' he had written in 1937, 'so for the same reason it is now advisable that they should incline to the opposite policy.'[25]

This opposite policy was to be the shape of the future. Once back in the Treasury himself, Keynes happily watched the 1941 budget implement his fiscal strategy of using taxation not just to raise revenue but to regulate aggregate demand in the economy as a whole. He told his mother that, having 'got my way on a number of points as much as is good for me', he attached most importance to its logical structure, which he thought 'is really a revolution in public finance'.[26] He was to use much the same language in 1944 about the government's commitment to maintain a high and stable level of employment through such methods – 'an outstanding State Paper which, if one casts one's mind back ten years or so, represents a revolution in official opinion'.[27]

What Keynes meant by 'full employment' later became a controversial issue. In the *General Theory* it is defined as the point at which prices rather than output rise in response to any increase in effective demand. In practical terms, Keynes stuck to the sort of target level suggested in 'Can Lloyd George Do It?' in 1929 – around 5 per cent unemployment. This became the official target in the war years, though Keynes himself came to think that it might be pessimistic. He told Sir William Beveridge, whose famous proposals on social security he supported: 'No harm in aiming at 3 per cent unemployment, but I shall be surprised if we succeed.'[28] The official figures in Britain show levels around 2 per cent from 1947 to 1970, and only from 1976 did the annual average rise above 5 per cent. OECD figures, on a standard basis, show unemployment in Britain above 10 per cent from 1982 to 1987, and a peak American rate just under 10 per cent in 1982–3.[29]

It is not misplaced to talk of a Keynesian revolution in British economic policy. There was admittedly no Damascene conversion in the Treasury; instead, a wartime accommodation under the pragmatic eye of Sir Richard Hopkins to the thinking of their extraordinary temporary colleague. It was only after the war, and his own retirement, that Hopkins actually found time to read the

General Theory. He then thought it worth reading again. Probably the only person in the Treasury who had really mastered it was Keynes's old friend Ralph Hawtrey, who had naturally given his own twist to what the Treasury came to understand as Keynesianism. Though the *General Theory* had preached about keeping interest rates low and stable, Hawtrey had no time for this, and urged on his Treasury colleagues the option of a flexible monetary policy, applying deflationary or reflationary pressure as required.

In reference to the former Soviet Union, there is a familiar distinction between talking of theoretical Marxism and the 'actually existing socialism' that was the historical reality. Likewise, 'actually existing Keynesianism' in Britain in the 1950s and 1960s, though indeed macroeconomic, hardly had the authority of the *General Theory* for relying on two key policy instruments. One of these was the 'fine-tuning' of consumption through fiscal policy, which became the main plank in Conservative policy in the 1950s, especially under the premiership of Harold Macmillan, whose reputation as a maverick Keynesian pioneer was proudly guarded by the Prime Minister himself. An arm's-length fiscal policy was thus a happy compromise, keeping at bay unhappy pre-war memories of monetary disciplines, as canvassed by some Conservatives whom we could call proto-monetarists. 'I do hope that no Government speaker will use words implying that the Government subscribes to such antiquated doctrine,' Macmillan was warned by his confidant, Sir Roy Harrod.[30]

But the Conservatives did revive bank rate as a policy instrument. This was a second respect in which the postwar Keynesian consensus arguably departed from Keynes himself, who envisaged a stable rate of interest, fixed at a low level. Yet from the return to office of the Conservatives in 1951, fiscal policy was co-ordinated with the manipulation of monetary policy through variable interest rates. Bank rate, which had been set continuously since 1932 (except for two months at the outbreak of war) at only

2 per cent, was first raised above this level on 8 November 1951, less than two weeks after the general election, and thereafter was used to enforce credit squeezes, with rates in double figures by the 1970s. Labour, which might well have done the same anyway if re-elected, subsequently followed suit. The *General Theory* had gone no further than conceding that there was 'force in the argument that a high rate of interest is much more effective against a boom than a low rate of interest against a slump'.[31] Thus pulling on a piece of string remained a more viable option than pushing on it.

And what about budget deficits in this period? To identify the balanced budget doctrine as the prime casualty of Keynes's teaching seems dubious, and to mourn its passing pointless. If there were persistent deficits in American budgets from the 1960s, it may have seemed tempting to attribute this to the supposition that 'the Keynesian theory of economic policy produces inherent biases when applied within the institutions of political democracy'.[32] But this surely claims either too much or too little. Too much, because if such tendencies are universal, democracy will presumably overthrow any balanced budget convention, Keynes or no Keynes. Too little, though, because the supporting evidence in fact seems to be restricted to American experience.

The British experience was otherwise. During the heyday of the Keynesian consensus, the budget was in fact in surplus in every year from 1948 to 1972, as measured by the conventional standards for a balanced budget since the time of Gladstone.[33] If there were subsequent fiscal problems, perhaps more immediate causes should be sought. Conversely, perhaps we should look to the specifically American institutions and conventions of governance to explain the workings of a congressional system that has undeniably fostered spending bills that cater to special interests. Once more, the different trajectory of British and American Keynesianism illustrates the perils of sweeping generalisations that ignore actual historical experience.

There is another way of looking at the whole issue of public spending and public debt. This too can be illustrated from official British government statistics.[34] In 1914 the British national debt amounted to 29 per cent of GDP; by 1920 it was 148 per cent. The World War was responsible for a burden that made inter-war chancellors 'slaves to the debt' and led them into frantic efforts, especially in 1931, to balance the budget at all costs. Yet twenty years of Treasury frugality only succeeded in reducing the national debt by 1940 to 136 per cent of GDP. Whereupon the Second World War – financed this time on basically Keynesian lines – pushed up the debt, not this time by 520 per cent in real terms as in the First World War, but by 80 per cent.

The burden of internal debt that the British government carried in 1945 was thus 240 per cent of GDP. But postwar chancellors, no longer slaves to the debt in an era of alleged Keynesian profligacy, had different priorities, notably economic growth. The results are sobering, one way or another. By 1965 the national debt was only 96 per cent of GDP; by 1980 it had been halved again, down to 48 per cent, and was at much the same level at the end of the century. The reason, of course, is not that the debt itself had declined; indeed at current prices the outstanding debt nominally on the books in 1945 (£21,366 million) was twenty times greater by 2000. The real reason was, of course, the growth of GDP meanwhile – more than a hundred times greater at current prices over the same period. Some of this was inflation, but the real burden of the debt had none the less been reduced by 80 per cent. The actual moral seems to be twofold. First, be wary of expensive wars, especially if financed through debt rather than taxation. Secondly, that by looking after output and employment, it was indeed true, as Keynes had put it in 1934, that the budget could look after itself.

'I am a highly teachable person,' Keynes said on one occasion in 1940. 'I learn from criticism and before now have laid myself open to the reproof that my second thoughts are often better than my first thoughts – which is an indication, some people think, of a dangerous instability of character.'[35] He did not cling to hidebound texts in face of changing circumstances, he thought that there were worse offences than heresy and he recognised a need in every generation for fresh thinking about the agenda of economic policy.

There is no single, static, canonical version of Keynes's thought. After the *General Theory*, as before it, he refused to act as the pope of a new religion. This is one reason why there is legitimate ground for taking different views of his legacy. The varieties of Keynesianism that subsequently flourished – and sometimes withered – were attempts to extend his ideas in trying to make them operational. These were not the first doctrines to find their hubris met by nemesis as history unfolded.

We certainly ought to have qualms about too readily invoking the name of an economist who, for more than sixty years, has been unable to defend himself or clarify the meaning of his ideas. We do not need the sort of anachronistic ventriloquism that is liable to be displayed if we keep asking, what would Keynes think today? Austin Robinson, who knew him well as a senior colleague, wrote in 1947 that it was 'an effort to realise that Keynes, who was in the 1930s so utterly of the younger generation', had watched the funeral of Queen Victoria and still manifested traits which seemed 'almost Victorian'.[36] Personally, in talking with Sir Austin nearly forty years later, I naturally regarded this spry nonagenarian in his tennis shoes as himself a figure from a distant era, seemingly remote from some of our current concerns – and the world has moved on since then, of course.

Keynes's legacy to the study of economics goes beyond doctrinal disputes. The development of national income accounting, building on pioneering work by the American Simon Kuznets, had an obvious Keynesian thrust but nobody today regards concepts like national income, gross national product (GNP) or gross domestic product (GDP) as ideologically charged or tainted. In establishing a macroeconomic approach, Keynes was setting up a framework of analysis within which non-Keynesian economists could later work too. Perhaps this is what Friedman meant in saying: 'In one sense, we are all Keynesians now; in another, nobody is any longer a Keynesian.'[37]

We can still benefit from some of Keynes's central theoretical insights. We can recognise not only that expectations are crucial, but that they are often circular and self-fulfilling, for good or ill. We can recognise that there are problems that the market cannot sort out for us, when our individual urges to protect ourselves become self-defeating. And we can recognise that government, far from being the problem, is a necessary part of the solution.

Keynes's understanding of the mass psychology of confidence has again come into its own in an era that has suddenly lost confidence. On Wall Street during the boom years, the 'masters of the universe' certainly exhibited enough animal spirits to fill a good-sized zoo; but that was yesterday and the hangover from such excess is with us today. Perhaps the markets can be relied upon to bounce back in the long run but such spontaneous resilience, as I write, seems to be in short supply. We can see that there is a tipping point in the economic cycle when the market is not simply undergoing a correction, but over-correcting in a spiral that drags us all down – unless we decide collectively to take counter-measures.

Keynes's thinking can still help us confront problems that have some unnerving echoes, parallels and relevance in the world that we live in today. If we recognise the sort of trouble we face, we may be able to devise specific solutions, as Keynes did in his own day. As we have seen, Keynes regarded budget deficits as a lesser evil in a slump, and conversely advocated a budget surplus when inflation threatened. He may well have underestimated the difficulties of timing public investment so as to produce the appropriate counter-cyclical effects.

He may have been too sceptical about the effectiveness of stimulating consumption during a recession. He may latterly have underestimated the effectiveness of monetary policy, at least in its disciplinary role in checking a boom. He had as few effective answers as later Keynesians to some of the problems of reconciling full employment with the restraint of inflation.

Keynes was himself a liberal who believed that political reform was both possible and desirable. His support for the New Deal was not just a matter of economic technique. 'You remain for me the ruler whose general outlook and attitude to the tasks of government are the most sympathetic in the world,' he stated in his public endorsement of Roosevelt in 1933. He commended the President for 'feeling your way by trial and error', and supported both the recovery policies and the reform measures of the New Deal. 'In my country, as in your own, your position remains singularly untouched by criticism of this or the other detail,' Keynes declared. 'Our hope and our faith are based on broader considerations.'[38]

Like Keynes, people today may believe that the United States has lessons to teach – but perhaps also to learn – about the compatibility of recovery and reform. Keynes's own support for the principles of the welfare state, as introduced in Britain in the 1940s, partly rested on his belief in the self-compensating effects of preventing incomes, and therefore demand, from collapsing in a depression. Even today, there is an instructive contrast between the ongoing support enjoyed by unemployed workers in most European countries (likewise in Canada) and the plight of American workers who often lose their health insurance along with their jobs. Of course this consequently produces relatively larger deficits in European budgets, and thus exerts an *automatic* stabilising effect lacking in the United States. It may be no coincidence that Germany and France, with the best public health-care systems in Europe, have been relatively chary in signing up to the sort of specific, one-off stimulus package that is felt necessary in the United States.

John Maynard Keynes was inconsistent far less often than is alleged. But he was guilty of changing his mind – usually for the better. What reason do we have for supposing that he would have denied us similar licence? In policy, we are surely not wrong, more than seventy years after his *General Theory*, to improvise particular measures appropriate to our own times. Keynes's name is thus rightly invoked to license fresh approaches to the novel economic difficulties of our own era – to tackle them actively rather than take refuge in inert doctrinal purity.

It is indeed Keynesian to applaud government for trying something, and on a large scale too, when faced with obvious market failure. And the yardstick that Keynes introduced for assessing the costs is still valid: whether the economy itself can be expanded by such measures, generating the very resources that finance the initial stimulus. That is what justifies government action, not only for reasons of short-term expediency, but also in the long run.

Acknowledgements

On 8 January 2009 a seminal op-ed article on Keynes appeared worldwide in the distinctive pink pages of the *Financial Times*. I know that it was seminal because the piece that I wrote then became the seed of this book – germinated almost as soon as it had been first touched by the green fingers of my wife, Maria Tippett, and energetically propagated when it then passed into the hands of my two editors at Bloomsbury, Peter Ginna in New York and Michael Fishwick in London. I thank them all for backing this project in the first place and for responding with much-needed support and encouragement during the intensive weeks of composition. The first steps were taken while Maria and I were Director's Visitors at the Institute for Advanced Study at Princeton in January and February 2009. When I confessed to the Director, Dr Peter Goddard, that I was now working on a completely different topic from the one that I had specified in advance, he immediately assured me that this was in the best traditions of the Institute – a daunting standard, of course. And the past years of research on which I drew in writing this completely new treatment of the historical Keynes and the impact of Keynesian economics have continued to be supported in the economist's own university by St John's College, where I was a Fellow for twenty years, and by Trinity Hall, Cambridge, where I was later Master and am now grateful to be an Honorary Fellow. But the furious activity of actually writing the book exploited the tranquillity of the house, studio and library that Maria and I have built on Pender Island, British Columbia. My words were faithfully scrutinised, on the spot by Maria and the Canadian literary scholar Paul Delany, and electronically by my old friends in England, Stefan Collini, John Thompson and Richard Toye. Their suggestions made for a better submission to Bloomsbury, where not only Peter Ginna and Michael Fishwick but also my managing editor, Anna Simpson, copy-editor Jenny Overton and indexer Alan Rutter, proved indefatigable in meeting an unforgiving deadline. With so much help in its making, this book ought to be the perfect introduction to a topic of inexhaustible fascination; and any shortcomings are simply my own.

Peter Clarke
Pender Island, June 2009

Bibliography

Donald Moggridge (with Sir Austin Robinson), *The Collected Writings of John Maynard Keynes*, 30 vols. (Cambridge University Press for the Royal Economic Society): cited as *JMK*, with volume number in roman numerals, followed by page references, to the following volumes:

JMK, I, *Indian Currency and Finance* (1913)

JMK, II: *The Economic Consequences of the Peace* (1919)

JMK, III: *A Revision of the Treaty* (1922)

JMK, IV: *A Tract on Monetary Reform* (1923)

JMK, V and VI: *A Treatise on Money* (1930)

JMK, VII: *The General Theory of Employment, Interest and Money* (1936)

JMK, VIII: *A Treatise on Probability* (1921)

JMK, IX: *Essays in Persuasion* (1931 text plus additions including pamphlets)

JMK, X, *Essays in Biography* (1933 text plus additions)

JMK, XI: Academic economic articles

JMK, XII: Investment and editorial material

JMK, XIII–XXVII and XXIX: activities, including correspondence and drafts

JMK, XXVIII: social, political and literary writings

JMK, XXX: bibliography and index.

This magnificent edition is indispensable. I list below all other works cited in the endnotes by short titles only. Place of publication is always London (and usually New York too) unless otherwise specified; university presses are simply given as such; and separate paperback editions likewise. I have also bestowed an asterisk on a dozen books, recommended for further reading. These were selected either because they were written by me or to offer a small repayment on debts which a different kind of book would have acknowledged in traditional academic footnotes.

Annual Abstract of Statistics (Her Majesty's Stationery Office, 2001 edn.).

Badger, Anthony J., *The New Deal: The depression years, 1933–40* (1989).

Barber, William J., 'Government as a laboratory under Roosevelt', see Furner and Supple (eds.), *The State and Economic Knowledge*.

*Bateman, Bradley W., *Keynes's Uncertain Revolution* (University of Michigan Press, 1996).

Biagini, Eugenio, 'Keynesian ideas and the recasting of Italian democracy, 1945–53', see Green and Tanner (eds.), *Strange Survival*.

Brittan, Samuel, *The Treasury under the Tories* (Penguin edn., 1964).

Brooke, Christopher, *A History of the University of Cambridge*, vol. IV (Cambridge University Press, 1993).

Brown, Neville, *Dissenting Forebears: The maternal ancestors of J. M. Keynes* (Chichester, Sx, 1988).

Buchanan, James M., John Burton and Richard E. Wagner, *The Consequences of Mr Keynes* (London, Institute of Economic Affairs, 1978).

Buchanan, James M. and Richard E. Wagner, *Democracy in Deficit: The political legacy of Lord Keynes* (1977).

*Carabelli, Anna M., *On Keynes's Method* (1988).

*Clarke, Peter, *The Keynesian Revolution in the Making, 1924–1936* (Oxford University Press, 1988).

*Clarke, Peter, *The Keynesian Revolution and its Economic Consequences* (Cheltenham, Glos.; Northampton, Mass., 1998).

Clarke, Peter, *The Last Thousand Days of the British Empire* (Penguin, 2007).

Collins, Robert M., 'The emergence of economic growthmanship in the US', see Furner and Supple (eds.), *The State and Economic Knowledge*.

Congdon, Tim, *Reflections on Monetarism* (London, Institute of Economic Affairs, 1992) for essay from *Encounter* (April 1975).

Crosland, C. A. R., 'The transition from capitalism', see Crossman (ed.), *Essays*.

Crossman, R. H. S. (ed.), *New Fabian Essays* (1952) for essay by C. A. R. Crosland, 'The transition from capitalism'.

De Cecco, Marcello, 'Keynes and Italian economics', see Hall (ed.), *Political Power*.

Deutscher, Patrick, *R. G. Hawtrey and the Development of Macroeconomics* (1990).

*Dimand, Robert W., *The Origins of the Keynesian Revolution: The development of Keynes's theory of employment and output* (Aldershot, Hants., 1988).

Eatwell, John and Murray Milgate, *Keynes's Economics and the Theory of Value and Distribution* (1983).

Fitzgibbons, Athol, *Keynes's Vision: A new political economy* (Oxford University Press, 1988).

Friedman, Milton, 'The role of monetary policy', *American Economic Review*, LVIII (1968), pp. 1–17.

Furner, Mary and Barry Supple (eds.), *The State and Economic Knowledge: The American and British experience* (Woodrow Wilson International Center and Cambridge University Press, 1990) for William J. Barber, 'Government as a laboratory under Roosevelt'; Robert M. Collins, 'The emergence of economic growthmanship in the US'; George C. Peden, 'Old dogs and new tricks: the British Treasury'.

Galbraith, John Kenneth, 'How Keynes came to America', see Keynes, Milo (ed.), *Essays*.

Galbraith, John Kenneth, *The Great Crash, 1929* (Penguin edn., 1961).

Gardner, Richard N., *Sterling-Dollar Dipomacy in Current Perspective* (Columbia University Press, 1988).

Green, Ewen, 'The Conservative Party and Keynes', see Green and Tanner (eds.), *Strange Survival*.

Green, E. H. H. and Tanner, D. M. (eds.), *The Strange Survival of Liberal England* (Cambridge University Press, 2007) for Richard Toye, 'The Labour Party and Keynes'; Ewen Green, 'The Conservative Party and Keynes'; Eugenio Biagini, 'Keynesian ideas and the recasting of Italian democracy, 1945–53'.

Hadley, Eleanor M., 'The diffusion of Keynesian ideas in Japan', see Hall (ed.), *Political Power*.

Hall, Peter A. (ed.), *The Political Power of Economic Ideas: Keynesianism across nations* (Princeton University Press, 1989) for Walter S. Salant, 'The spread of Keynesian ideas and practices in the United States'; Pierre Rosanvallon, 'The development of Keynesianism in France'; Marcello de Cecco, 'Keynes and Italian economics'; Harold James, 'What is Keynesian about deficit financing? The case of inter-war Germany'; and Eleanor M. Hadley, 'The diffusion of Keynesian ideas in Japan'.

*Harrod, Roy, *The Life of John Maynard Keynes* (1951).

Hawtrey, R. G., *The Art of Central Banking* (1932).

Hayek, F. A., *Tiger by the Tail: A 40 years' running commentary on Keynesianism by Hayek*, compiled by Sudha R. Shenoy, 2nd edn. (London, Institute of Economic Affairs, 1978).

Healey, Denis, *The Time of My Life* (1989).

Hill, Polly and Richard Keynes (eds.), *Lydia and Maynard: Letters between Lydia Lopokova and John Maynard Keynes* (1989).

Hogg, Quintin, *The Case for Conservatism* (Penguin, 1947).

Holroyd, Michael, *Lytton Strachey: A biography* (revised Penguin edn., 1979).

Howson, Susan and Donald Moggridge (eds.), *The Wartime Diaries of Lionel Robbins and James Meade, 1943–5* (1990).

*Howson, Susan and Donald Winch, *The Economic Advisory Council, 1930–1939: A study in economic advice during depression and recovery* (Cambridge University Press, 1977).

Hubback, D., *No Ordinary Press Baron: A life of Walter Layton* (1985).

Hutchison, T. W., *Keynes versus the 'Keynesians'* (London, Institute of Economic Affairs, 1977).

James, Harold, 'What is Keynesian about deficit financing? The case of inter-war Germany', see Hall (ed.), *Political Power*.

Johnson, Christopher, *The Economy under Mrs Thatcher, 1979–90* (Penguin, 1991).

Jones, Thomas, *A Diary with Letters, 1931–1950* (Oxford University Press, 1954).

Keynes, Geoffrey, 'The early years', see Keynes, Milo (ed.), *Essays*.

Keynes, Milo (ed.), *Essays on John Maynard Keynes* (Cambridge University Press, 1975) for essays by Geoffrey Keynes, 'The early years'; James Meade, 'The Keynesian revolution'; Joan Robinson, 'What has become of the Keynesian revolution?'; John Kenneth Galbraith, 'How Keynes came to America'.

Klein, Lawrence R., *The Keynesian Revolution* (1952).

Lawson, Nigel, *The View from No. 11* (1992) for 'The New Conservatism' (1980).

Lee, Hermione, *Virginia Woolf* (1996).

Lloyd George, David, *War Memoirs*, 2 vol. edn. (1938).

McCraw, Thomas, *Prophet of Innovation: Joseph Schumpeter and creative destruction* (Harvard University Press, 2007).

Meade, James, 'The Keynesian revolution', see Milo Keynes (ed.), *Essays*.

Middleton, Roger, *Government versus the Market: The growth of the public sector, economic management and British economic performance, c. 1890–1979* (Cheltenham, Glos.; Brookfield, Vt. US, 1996).

Mitchell, B. R., *British Historical Statistics* (Cambridge University Press, 1988).

*Moggridge, D. E., *British Monetary Policy, 1924–1931: The Norman Conquest of $4.86* (Cambridge University Press, 1972).

*Moggridge, D. E., *Maynard Keynes: An economist's biography* (1992).

Moran, Lord, *Churchill: Taken from the diaries of Lord Moran* (Boston, Mass., 1966).

Moran, Lord, *Churchill: The struggle for survival, 1945–60* (2006).

*O'Donnell, R. M., *Keynes: Philosophy, economics and politics* (1989).

Parker, John, *Labour Marches On* (Penguin, 1947).

Patinkin, Don, *Anticipations of the General Theory?* (University of Chicago, 1982).

Peden, George C., 'Old dogs and new tricks: the British Treasury', see Furner and Supple (eds.), *The State and Economic Knowledge*.

Peden, G. C. (ed.), *Keynes and his Critics: Treasury responses to the Keynesian revolution, 1925–1946* (Oxford University Press for the British Academy, 2004).

Robinson, E. A. G., 'John Maynard Keynes, 1883–1946', *Economic Journal*, LVII (1947), pp. 1–68.

Robinson, Joan, 'What has become of the Keynesian revolution', see Keynes, Milo (ed.), *Essays*.

Rosanvallon, Pierre, 'The development of Keynesianism in France', see Hall (ed.), *Political Power*.

Russell, Bertrand, *Autobiography*, 3 vols. (1967–9).

Rymes, Thomas K. (ed.), *Keynes's Lectures, 1932–35: Notes of a representative student* (London, Royal Economic Society, 1989).

Salant, Walter S., 'The spread of Keynesian ideas and practices in the United States', see Hall (ed.), *Political Power*.

Schlesinger, Arthur M., Jr, *A Thousand Days: John F. Kennedy in the White House* (Boston, Mass., 1965).

Schumpeter, Joseph, *Ten Great Economists; From Marx to Keynes* (1952).

Shackle, G. L. S., *The Years of High Theory: Invention and tradition in economic thought, 1926–1939* (Cambridge University Press, 1967).

*Skidelsky, Robert, *John Maynard Keynes*, 3 vols. (1983–2000).

Stansky, Peter and William Abrahams, *Journey to the Frontier: Julian Bell and John Cornford* (1966).

Stein, Herbert, *The Fiscal Revolution in America: Policy in pursuit of reality*, 2nd edn. (Washington, DC, American Enterprise Institute, 1996).

Straight, Michael, *After Long Silence* (1983).

Thatcher, Margaret, *Complete Public Statements, 1945–1990 on CD-ROM* (Oxford University Press, 1999) with Unique Document Number (UDN).

Toye, Richard, 'Keynes, the Labour movement and "How to Pay for the War", *Twentieth Century British History*, X (1999), pp. 255–81.

Toye, Richard, 'The Labour Party and Keynes', see Green and Tanner (eds), *Strange Survival*.

Toye, Richard, 'The trials of a biographer: Roy Harrod's *Life of John Maynard Keynes* reconsidered', see Toye and Gottlieb (eds.), *Making Reputations*.

Toye, Richard and Julie Gottlieb (eds.), *Making Reputations: Power, persuasion and the individual in modern British politics* (2005) for Richard Toye, 'The trials of a biographer: Roy Harrod's *Life of John Maynard Keynes* reconsidered', pp. 123–34.

*Winch, Donald, *Economics and Policy: A historical study* (Fontana edn., 1972).

Woolf, Leonard, *Sowing: An autobiography of the years 1880–1904* (1960).

Woolf, Virginia, *The Diary of Virginia Woolf*, ed. Anne Olivier Bell, 5 vols. (Penguin edn., 1977).

Notes

Notes to Introduction

1 Francis V. Greene in *New York Times*, 28 March 1920.
2 Harrod, *Keynes*, p. 396.
3 *JMK*, IV, 65.
4 8 October 1982, Thatcher, *Complete Public Statements*, UDN 82–276.
5 *JMK*, XX, 363–4.
6 Jones, *Diary*, p. 19.
7 Lloyd George, *War Memoirs*, I, p. 410.
8 *JMK*, XXI, 273–7.
9 *JMK*, XXI, 289.
10 McCraw, *Prophet of Innovation*, p. 274.
11 Galbraith in M. Keynes (ed.), *Essays*, p. 136.
12 Hogg, *Case for Conservatism*, pp. 219, 224.
13 Parker, *Labour Marches On*, p. 55.
14 Skidelsky, *Keynes*, III, p. 472.
15 Crosland in Crossman (ed.), *New Fabian Essays*, pp. 39–40.
16 Toye in Toye and Gottlieb (eds.), *Making Reputations*, p. 217, n. 2.
17 Brittan, *Treasury under the Tories*, p. 162.
18 Schlesinger, *Thousand Days*, p. 630.
19 Heller cited, *Time*, 25 November 1966.
20 *JMK*, VII, 383–4.
21 *Time*, 31 December 1965.
22 *Time*, 4 February 1966 (letters).

23 *New York Times*, 6 and 10 January 1971.
24 Friedman, 'Role', *American Economic Review*, LVIII, p. 3.
25 *Time*, 10 January 1969.
26 Healey, *Time of My Life*, p. 378.
27 Congdon, essay, *Reflections on Monetarism*, p. 198.
28 Lawson, *View from No. 11*, p. 1041.
29 Thatcher, *Complete Public Statements*, UDN 79–443.
30 Thatcher, *Complete Public Statements*, UDN 84–270.
31 Thatcher, *Complete Public Statements*, UDN, 85–121.
32 Thatcher, *Complete Public Statements*, UDN 82–231.
33 *Time*, 17 January 1983.
34 Quoted by Toye in Green and Tanner (eds.), *Strange Survival*, p. 184.
35 *Guardian*, 20 October 2008.
36 *Time*, 23 October 2008.

Notes to Chapter 1

1   Moggridge, *Keynes*, p. 16.
2   Harrod, *Keynes*, pp. 2, 80, 192–3.
3   Moggridge, *Keynes*, p. 96.
4   *JMK*, X, 173.
5   Moggridge, *Keynes*, p. 108.
6   Hubback, *Layton*, p. 77.
7   *Oxford Dictionary of Quotations*.
8   Moggridge, *Keynes*, p. 187.
9   *JMK*, X, 446.
10 Moggridge, *Keynes*, pp. 838–9.
11 V. Woolf, *Diary*, V, pp. 168–9.
12 *JMK*, X, 446.
13 *JMK*, X, 446.
14 L. Woolf, *Sowing*, p. 148.
15 Robinson, 'Keynes', *Economic Journal*, LVII, pp. 10, 25.
16 *JMK*, VII, 334.
17 *JMK*, XVI, 296–7.
18 Holroyd, *Strachey*, p. 598.
19 *JMK*, XVI, 178.
20 Holroyd, *Strachey*, pp. 628–9.
21 *JMK*, II, 89–90.

22 *JMK*, XVII, 15; *JMK*, II, 91.

23 *JMK*, III, 2.

24 Moggridge, *Keynes*, p. 312.

25 *JMK*, XVI, 460.

26 *JMK*, II, 189.

27 Brooke, *Cambridge*, IV, pp. 281–7.

28 Brown, *Dissenting Forebears*, p. 142.

29 Lee, *Virginia Woolf*, pp. 556–8.

30 Holroyd, *Strachey*, p. 733 n.

31 *JMK*, II, 18, 20.

32 *JMK*, II, 24, 26.

33 *JMK*, II, 26.

34 *JMK*, II, 26.

35 *JMK*, II, 34.

36 *JMK*, X, 196.

37 *JMK*, X, 39.

38 *JMK*, XII, tables at 2, 11.

Notes to Chapter 2

1   G. Keynes in M. Keynes (ed.), *Essays*, p. 27.

2   Skidelsky, *Keynes*, II, pp. 100–1.

3   Moggridge, *Keynes*, p. 285.

4   Moggridge, *Keynes*, p. 395.

5   Hill and Keynes (eds.), *Lydia and Maynard*, p. 31.

6   V. Woolf, *Diary*, II, p. 266.

7   V. Woolf, *Diary*, III, p. 181.

8   Skidelsky, *Keynes*, II, p. 303.

9   Moggridge, *Keynes*, p. 586.

10 *JMK*, IX, 328–9.

11 *JMK*, XXI, 237.

12 *JMK*, XXI, 242.

13 *JMK*, XXI, 236.

14 Moggridge, *Keynes*, p. 705.

15 *JMK*, XXI, 244.

16 Hill and Keynes (eds.), *Lydia and Maynard*, p. 36.

17 Hill and Keynes (eds.), *Lydia and Maynard*, p. 130.

18 *JMK*, II, 148.

19 Hill and Keynes (eds.), *Lydia and Maynard*, p. 138.
20 *JMK*, IX, 296–7.
21 Mitchell, *British Historical Statistics*, p. 124.
22 *JMK*, XIX, 219–23.
23 Hill and Keynes (eds.), *Lydia and Maynard*, p. 205.
24 *JMK*, XIX, 639–40.
25 *JMK*, IX, 294.
26 *JMK*, XIX, 222.
27 *JMK*, IX, 309.
28 *JMK*, XXI, 236.
29 *JMK*, XXI, 239.
30 Stansky and Abrahams, *Journey to the Frontier*, pp. 108–9.
31 *JMK*, XXVIII, 38.
32 *JMK*, XXI, 246.
33 Skidelsky, *Keynes*, III, p. 11.
34 *JMK*, XXI, 494–5.
35 *JMK*, IX, xvii.
36 *JMK*, XXVIII, 36.
37 *JMK*, XXI, 372–3.
38 *JMK*, X, 447–8.
39 *JMK*, III, 3.
40 *JMK*, XXVIII, 35.
41 *JMK*, XXVIII, 42.
42 *JMK*, VII, xxi.
43 Skidelsky, *Keynes*, III, p. 87.
44 *JMK*, XXII, 38.
45 *JMK*, XXII, 149.
46 Moggridge, *Keynes*, p. 638.
47 Skidelsky, *Keynes*, III, p. 265.
48 Howson and Moggridge (eds.), *Wartime Diaries*, p. 100.
49 *JMK*, XXIII, 107.
50 Clarke, *Last Thousand Days*, p. xvii.
51 Howson and Moggridge (eds.), *Wartime Diaries*, pp. 133, 135.
52 *JMK*, XIX, 160.
53 Gardner, *Sterling-Dollar Diplomacy*, p. 97.
54 *JMK*, XXIV, 188 (Frank Lee).
55 *Financial Times*, 23 March 2009.
56 Clarke, *Last Thousand Days*, pp. 313, 370.

57 Moggridge, *Keynes*, p. 798.
58 Harrod, *Keynes*, p. 596.
59 Gardner, *Sterling-Dollar Diplomacy*, p. xiii.
60 *JMK*, XXIV, 610, 621.
61 *JMK*, V, 11–12.

Notes to Chapter 3

1 Harrod, *Keynes*, p. 618.
2 Russell, *Autobiography*, I, p. 72.
3 Howson and Moggridge (eds.), *Wartime Diaries*, pp. 158–9.
4 Galbraith, *Great Crash*, pp. 127–8.
5 Clarke, *Keynesian Revolution in the Making*, pp. 103, 105.
6 *JMK*, XIX, 223.
7 *Financial Times*, 2 April 2009; cf. Mitchell, *British Historical Statistics*, pp. 581–95; *JMK*, IX, 92–3.
8 *JMK*, IV, 61.
9 *JMK*, IV, 65.
10 Schumpeter, *Ten Great Economists*, p. 275.
11 *JMK*, IV, 56–7.
12 *JMK*, XXI, 239.
13 Moggridge, *British Monetary Policy*, pp. 76, 266.
14 *JMK*, IV, 56.
15 Moggridge, *British Monetary Policy*, p. 272.
16 *JMK*, XX, 86.
17 *JMK*, VI, 132.
18 *JMK*, VI, 137.
19 *JMK*, VI, 163.
20 *JMK*, XX, 87.
21 *JMK*, XX, 53–4.
22 *Nation*, 24 January 1931.
23 Moran, *Churchill from the diaries*, p. 330; Moran, *Churchill: Struggle for Survival*, p. 326.
24 *JMK*, IX, 212.
25 *JMK*, IX, 224.
26 Peden, *Keynes and his Critics*, p. 43.
27 *JMK*, IX, 224.
28 *JMK*, XX, 79.

29 *JMK*, IV, 138.

30 *JMK*, VI, 337.

31 *JMK*, XX, 85.

32 *JMK*, XI, 458.

33 Peden, *Keynes and his Critics*, p. 46.

34 QQ. 3319, 3328, 3338–9, 3345–7, 3390–1, 3498 (Clarke, *Keynesian Revolution in the Making*, pp. 126–8).

35 Clarke, *Keynesian Revolution in the Making*, p. 104.

36 *JMK*, XX, 126, 129, 146–7.

37 *JMK*, XX, 125.

38 *JMK*, XX, 375.

39 *JMK*, IX, 122, 124.

40 *JMK*, IX, 125.

41 *The Times*, 16 April 1929.

42 *JMK*, XX, 129–30.

43 Peden, *Keynes and his Critics*, p. 103.

44 Peden, *Keynes and his Critics*, p. 95 n.

45 *JMK*, XX, 168–9.

46 QQ. 5410, 5413, 5450 (Clarke, *Keynesian Revolution in the Making*, p. 150).

47 *JMK*, XX, 166, 168.

48 *JMK*, XX, 172.

49 *JMK*, XX, 179.

50 Harrod, *Keynes*, p. 422.

51 *JMK*, XX, 357–60.

52 Hawtrey, *Art of Central Banking*, p. 271.

53 QQ. 4257, 4275, 4239 (Clarke, *Keynesian Revolution in the Making*, p. 146).

54 QQ. 6648, 6658 (Clarke, *Keynesian Revolution in the Making*, pp. 179–80).

55 *The Times*, 6 June 1930.

56 Howson and Winch, *Economic Advisory Council*, p. 229.

57 Middleton, *Government versus the Market*, p. 388.

Notes to Chapter 4

1 *JMK*, XX, 86.

2 *JMK*, XX, 87.

3 *JMK*, XX, 350–1.
4 *JMK*, XIII, 176.
5 Hayek, *Tiger by the Tail*, p. 100.
6 *JMK*, XIII, 172.
7 *JMK*, XXIX, 270.
8 Q. 4834 (Clarke, *Keynesian Revolution in the Making*, p. 171).
9 *JMK*, XIV, 94.
10 *JMK*, XIII, 229, 230.
11 *JMK*, XIII, 243.
12 Hawtrey, *Art of Central Banking*, par. 374.
13 Rymes (ed.), *Keynes's Lectures*, p. 61.
14 *JMK*, XIII, 275–6.
15 *JMK*, XXIX, 270.
16 *JMK*, XIX, 202 n. 2.
17 *JMK*, xiv, 94–5.
18 Robinson, 'Keynes', *Economic Journal*, LVII, p. 67.
19 *JMK*, IX, 106.
20 Meade in M. Keynes (ed.), *Essays*, p. 82.
21 J. Robinson in M. Keynes (ed.), *Essays*, p. 125.
22 *JMK*, XX, 76–8.
23 *JMK*, XIV, 85.
24 *JMK*, XIV, 211.
25 *JMK*, XIV, 85.
26 Straight, *After Long Silence*, p. 57.
27 Rymes (ed.), *Keynes's Lectures*, p. 69.
28 *JMK*, XX, 365.
29 *JMK*, XIV, 85.
30 Clarke, *Keynesian Revolution in the Making*, p. 268.
31 *JMK*, XXI, 149–51.
32 *JMK*, IX, 349–50.
33 *JMK*, XXI, 184.
34 Deutscher, *Hawtrey and Macroeconomics*, pp. 189–91.
35 *JMK*, XIII, 548.
36 *JMK*, VII, 85.
37 *JMK*, VII, 89.
38 *JMK*, VII, 131.
39 *JMK*, VII, 83.
40 *JMK*, VII, 365.

41 Clarke, *Keynesian Revolution and its Economic Consequences*, p. 116.
42 *JMK*, XIV, 113–14, 116.
43 *JMK*, VII, 148.
44 *JMK*, VII, 159.
45 *JMK*, VII, 161.
46 *JMK*, XII, 520.
47 *JMK*, VII, xxxii.
48 *JMK*, VII, xxiii.
49 *JMK*, XXIX, 165.
50 *JMK*, XIV, 100.

Notes to Epilogue

 1 *Guardian Weekly*, 10 April 2009.
 2 *JMK*, VII, xxxi.
 3 Rosanvallon in Hall (ed.), *Political Power of Economic Ideas*, p. 190.
 4 *JMK*, VII, xxv, xxix.
 5 Biagini in Green and Tanner (eds.), *Strange Survival*, pp. 227–8.
 6 Schumpeter, *Ten Great Economists*, pp. 274–5.
 7 Quoted by Winch, *Economics and Policy*, p. 260.
 8 Badger, *New Deal*, pp. 66, 111–12.
 9 *JMK*, XXI, 428.
10 *JMK*, XXI, 307.
11 *JMK*, XXIII, 155.
12 Barber in Furner and Supple (eds.), *State and Economic Knowledge*, p. 104.
13 Barber in Furner and Supple (eds.), *State and Economic Knowledge*, p. 121.
14 *JMK*, XXII, 149, quoted more fully in ch. 2.
15 Barber in Furner and Supple (eds.), *State and Economic Knowledge*, p.114 n.
16 Stein, *Fiscal Revolution in America*, p. 167.
17 A. Robinson in Hutchison, *Keynes versus the 'Keynesians'*, p. 58.
18 *JMK*, VII, 98.
19 *JMK*, VII, 128–9.
20 *JMK*, XXI, 308.
21 *JMK*, XXI, 337.
22 *JMK*, XXVII, 353–4.

23 *JMK*, XXVII, 319.

24 *JMK*, XXVII, 353.

25 *JMK*, XXI, 390.

26 *JMK*, XXII, 353–4.

27 *JMK*, XXVII, 364.

28 *JMK*, XXVII, 381.

29 Mitchell, *British Historical Statistics*, p. 124; Johnson, *Economy under Thatcher*, p. 315.

30 Green in Green and Tanner (eds.), *Strange Survival*, p. 201.

31 *JMK*, VII, 320.

32 Buchanan and Wagner, *Democracy in Deficit*, p. x.

33 Clarke, *Keynesian Revolution and its Economic Consequences*, pp. 210–12, which corrects misleading statistics in Buchanan, Burton and Wagner, *Consequences of Mr Keynes*.

34 Calculations from Mitchell, *British Historical Statistics*, pp. 602–3, 830–1; *Annual Abstract of Statistics*, tables 15.2, 17.7.

35 Toye, 'Keynes, Labour Movement and "How to Pay"', *Twentieth Century British History*, X, p. 271.

36 Robinson, *Economic Journal*, LVII, 7, p. 25.

37 *Time*, 4 February 1966; see introduction above for context.

38 *JMK*, XXI, 295.

Index

Page references in **bold** refer to illustrations

A NOTE ON THE TYPE

The text of this book is set in Granjon. This old-style face is named after the Frenchman Robert Granjon, a sixteenth-century letter cutter whose italic types have often been used with the romans of Claude Garamond. The origins of this face, like those of Garamond, lie in the late fifteenth century types used by Aldus Manutius in Italy.